A History of Colonial Education, 1607-1776

Studies in the History of American Education Series

Henry J. Perkinson
and Vincent P. Lannie
General Editors

Sheldon Cohen
A History of Colonial Education, 1607–1776
David Madsen
Early National Education, 1776–1830
Frederick M. Binder
The Age of the Common School, 1830–1865
Patricia Albjerg Graham
Community and Class in American Education, 1865–1918
Edgar Gumbert and Joel H. Spring
The Superschool and the Superstate:
American Education in the Twentieth Century, 1918–1970

A History of Colonial Education; 1607-1776

Sheldon S. Cohen
Loyola University

John Wiley & Sons, Inc., New York · London · Sydney · Toronto

Library of Congress Cataloging in Publication Data:

Cohen, Sheldon S
  A history of colonial education: 1607–1776

  (Studies in the history of American education series)
  Bibliography: p.
  1. Education—United States—History. I. Title.

LA206.C63 1974   370'.973   74–754
ISBN 0–471–16421–6
ISBN 0–471–16422–4 (pbk.)

Printed in the United States of America

10 9 8 7 6 5 4 3 2 1

series preface

This series provides new interpretations of American educational history based on the best recent scholarship. It contains five volumes that present, chronologically and topically, the history of American education from the beginning to the present day.

Each volume gives an original analysis and interpretation of the development of formal and informal agencies of education during a particular period.

Henry J. Perkinson

Library of Congress Cataloging in Publication Data:

Cohen, Sheldon S
  A history of colonial education: 1607–1776

  (Studies in the history of American education series)
  Bibliography: p.
  1. Education—United States—History. I. Title.

LA206.C63 1974   370'.973   74–754
ISBN 0–471–16421–6
ISBN 0–471–16422–4 (pbk.)

Printed in the United States of America

10 9 8 7 6 5 4 3 2 1

contents

A History of Colonial Education, 1607-1776

introduction

Writers who initially examined the foundations of the American educational system displayed remarkable talents at reproducing masses of factual material. Schoolbooks, school curricula, school laws, schoolteachers, and other aspects of colonial instruction were scrutinized and documented in great detail. This documentation generally offered a good factual recapitulation of the various institutional features of education in early America, but it missed the overall meaning of its subject. By excluding the broader social and cultural environment from their studies, these writers often gave a narrow, limited, and generally systemized perspective of the role of learning in early America. All too often, this circumscribed approach prevailed in teacher textbooks and training courses during the first part of this century. Recent decades, however, have witnessed a renewed interest in American educational foundations, and with this concern has emerged an expanded basis on which to examine this aspect of our nation's history.

Contemporary works concerning the educational patterns of early America generally regard their subject as an integral part of a broad social context. The present study follows a similar approach; it conceives of education as a reflection of society in colonial America; it attempts to show how education adjusted to the particular needs and conditions of this society; and it attempts to explain how educational changes in themselves contributed to a restructuring of colonial society. In chronological order, this study traces instructional practices in the colonies from their European, and particularly English, antecedents to the outbreak of the American Revolution. The subsequent educational patterns of the new nation rested heavily on this colonial cornerstone.

chapter one
european and english antecedents

the origins of American education lie in sixteenth- and early seventeenth-century Western Europe. Historians such as Edwin G. Dexter, who commenced his survey of colonial learning with the Jamestown settlement in 1607, ignored the basic heritage, institutions, and traditions that existed on the opposite side of the Atlantic. When European peoples expanded into the Americas, the various settlers transferred their Old World cultures along with their own particular motives for emigration to their new environments. Once established in the New World, the colonists attempted to reinstitute the most familiar institutions from their European past. Education was among the most important of the many social institutions that constituted this extensive cultural transplantation. If, therefore, we wish to understand the origins of education in the New World—principally among the English colonists—the true beginnings must first be observed within the context of their European and English antecedents.

Western Europe: 1500–1630

Economically and politically Western Europe found itself in a period of significant transformation at this time. Within the economic sphere, mercantile capitalism, with its accent on expanded commerce and profitable new markets, continued to displace the restrictive remnants of agrarian feudalism. Urban commercial centers (e.g., Brussels, Paris, Amsterdam, London), emphasizing trade, finance, and some industry, continued to expand and flourish. Discoveries of new sea-borne trade routes to Asia and the influx of riches from the New World had quickened the pace of this economic transformation—especially during the sixteenth century. By the close of this period, such broad, commercial changes, while neither total nor universal, had firmly altered the general economic structure of Western Europe.

A consolidation of centralized political states under energetic national monarchs—also taking place at this time—was linked directly to Western Europe's economic changes. As the area's local monarchs had expanded their power and authority over recalcitrant feudal lords, they found ready allies among urban merchants and bankers who frequently sought protection for their growing commercial ventures. By the early sixteenth century the achievement of a unified nation-state was virtually complete in England, France, Spain, and Portugal. There, autocratic monarchs demanded the political allegiance of the inhabitants, and they often directed the course of economic expansion into the unknown lands of the Far East and the New World.

The religious atmosphere of the sixteenth and early seventeenth centuries was more dramatic and certainly as meaningful as the previouly mentioned economic-political developments. In October 1517, Martin Luther sparked the ecclesiastical upheaval that soon split the existing unity of the Roman Catholic Church. The resultant religious revolt, whose intellectual origins could be traced prior to the Renaissance, brought forward many revolutionary concepts in theology. Its principal innovation, however, was the belief that salvation was an individual matter between God and man. For Protestant leaders such as Martin Luther and John Calvin, who denied Papal supremacy, God's saving grace was achieved by obedience to scriptural command rather than through the intermediary of a hierarchical church. Roman Catholics denied these radical concepts as heresy and belatedly attempted to mend the theological split with their Counter-Reformation. Although Protestant ranks were beset by several sectarian divisions, they proved able to survive the subsequent efforts of militant Catholic rulers and religious orders to restore a single universal church. By 1600, Lutheran, Calvinist, and smaller Anabaptist sects were still prevalent through much of Northern and Western Europe, while the Episcopal Church was solidly established in England. Even in Catholic nations such as France and Spain, autocratic monarchs had been able to transfer control of the secular clergy from the pope to the Monarch. Toleration of dissenters was almost nonexistent while bitter religious animosities continued long after the devasting Thirty Years War (1618–1648). Such theological developments were extremely significant to the American colonists who were quick to establish institutions for perpetuating their particular sectarian beliefs.

Europe's social structure underwent the least overt alterations in the era of colonization. Restrictive, sharply defined class lines from the medieval period persisted despite the losses of power sustained by feudal nobles and the effects of the Commercial Revolution. In much of Western Europe the bourgeoisie increased their numbers while in some areas a new class of landed gentry emerged as distinct from the more patrician landed aristocracy. But at the bottom of society—both in cities and on farms or manors—there still remained the overwhelming masses of illiterate peasants and unskilled workers. For them life continued in its endless squalid and wretched manner.

Education in Western Europe: 1500–1640

The educational features of Western Europe generally mirrored the existing conditions and societal needs of this period.

Their origins lay in the medieval world, and, by the seventeenth century, they still remained subject to a rigid, class-dominated, theologically oriented social structure. These general features, many of which were afterward transplanted in America, were observed within both the formal and informal patterns of learning common to the region.

Informal education at this time still centered initially and primarily around the family unit. (One French scholar, Philippe Aries, has even gone so far as to declare that by the seventeenth century, the family group occupied a foremost position among community institutions in Western Europe.) It was through the father, mother, or perhaps an older sibling that the infant first learned about his immediate physical environment. Later, it was from within this same family circle that he was given his first instruction in religion and morality. As the child reached the age to begin vocational training, his kinship group directed his initial activity. In Europe's rural and urban regions children of both sexes followed their elders' examples, performing the various chores necessary to maintain a subsistence level. While the immediate community might assist this overall process of vocational training, it was basically the family that directed the transmission of agrarian tasks or artisan skills to individual children. Even boys and girls whose parents apprenticed them to masters found that almost all their occupational instruction was given within the confines of their master's family. This preeminent family role in informal instruction was but one of the many transplanted educational features that continued throughout the entire colonial period.

The characteristics of formal education in Western Europe were more complex than this informal training, although both retained a similar circumscribed base. Despite some changes from the medieval period, there was still nothing in existence resembling a modern state-supported, nonsectarian public education system. The schools that operated at the elementary and secondary levels were generally restrictive in their enrollments and were governed primarily by sectarian precepts. Latin grammar schools, combining classical and Christian training, spread northward from their fifteenth century Italian origins; yet such institutions remained limited mainly to middle- and upper-class boys. Vernacular schools, writing schools, and guild schools increased in number within urban centers, but poorer children were normally excluded from their confines. Private tutors continued to offer the best individual training, although their efforts were, of course, restricted to children of the aristocrats. The result of these educational restrictions was apparent in the very low literacy rate throughout most of this region at the beginning of Europe's overseas expansion.

A growing number of self-contained universities capped this circumscribed educational structure, but most of them retained a strongly conservative orientation. These higher institutions of learning, which had originated in eleventh-century Italy, spread throughout much of the European continent during the succeeding centuries. Limited to a social and intellectual elite, they had been able to gain considerable autonomy from secular authority. The university's sectarian curriculum, however, still centered around the medieval concept of the Trivium (grammar, rhetoric, and logic) and the Quadrivium (arithmetic, astronomy, geometry, and music) known as the "seven liberal arts." While the infusion of elements of Renaissance humanism widened its narrow scholastic scope, this general curriculum, grounded in ancient Latin and Greek, was considered sufficient for a well-rounded higher education. Society as yet required no broad based or specialized studies in the vernacular from either its college graduates or from most of the faculties of these universities.

While the principal features of higher education remained unchanged throughout this period, there were a few significant changes in the characteristics of elementary and secondary education. The most noteworthy innovation took place on the elementary level, as a direct result of the Protestant Reformation. As previously mentioned, Martin Luther had stressed man's individual role in the process of obtaining salvation, and a basic part of this process was the ability to read the Scriptures in one's native tongue. Luther himself had translated the Bible into German in 1523, thereby freeing it from its former Latin confines. He followed this achievement with appeals for the establishment of "sectarian vernacular" schools where children would be taught to read the Bible in German and to recite the catechism of their faith. In addition, he set the tone for other Protestant reformers by stressing a divinely ordained need for such mass rudimentary religious training. For Luther it was both a parental and a community obligation to send all children to these schools. In a letter to the mayors and aldermen of German cities, he sternly condemned the failure to fulfill this obligation: "In my judgment there is no other outward offense that in the sight of God so heavily burdens the World, and deserves such heavy chastisement, as the need to educate children." The sectarian vernacular school soon became a feature not only in the existing Lutheran states of Germany, but its precepts were also adopted in other European lands where Protestant beliefs emerged triumphant from the Reformation.

England at the Onset of Colonization: 1580–1640

The preceding paragraphs formed a general sketch of the peoples of Western Europe and the prevalent educational patterns of the sixteenth and early seventeenth centuries. From within this overall context however, we center particularly on the English people and their educational structure in order to understand the society and the instructional patterns that were subsequently established in colonial America. Emigrants from Great Britain comprised over 90 percent of the migrants to the English colonies during the century following the initial Jamestown settlement, and they maintained this predominance throughout the entire colonial period. English language, customs, and traditions still distinguished the culture of the 13 colonies by the beginning of the American Revolution. The origins of this momentous transit of civilization across the Atlantic can be found in a study of England and her inhabitants during the half century before the "Great Migration" in 1630.

On the surface, English society during these years appeared quite well ordered and peaceful. The largely rural population grew from about 4.2 million in 1590 to almost 5.5 million in 1640, in spite of a high disease and infant mortality rate.

Clearly delineated, hierarchial social classes marked this steadily increasing population. At the peak of the societal structure were the landed aristocrats whose lineage often stretched back to the eleventh century Norman Conquest. Directly beneath them in rural England were the recently elevated landed gentry, while in the cities the gentry's counterparts were the wealthy although untitled class of merchants, artisans and bankers. Lawyers, physicians, vicars, teachers, and independent yeoman farmers were among the most prominent members of what might be called middle-class Englishmen. Below them were the masses of poor workingmen, tenant farmers, and tradesmen in the urban centers. The bottom of the social ladder consisted of beggars, squatters, and other indigent groups. Although England displayed greater social mobility, and more intermingling occurred within these class orders than in continental Europe, social tranquility remained unattained. In fact, the causes for several of the early seventeenth-century migrations can be traced to increasing crime, epidemics, famines, and rural disorders afflicting both middle- and lower-class Englishmen.

English governmental policies also led to restlessness in the latter part of this period. The Tudor dynasty had established the legalistic basis for a highly centralized government, and, during the reign of Elizabeth I (1558–1603), an intense national pride had developed toward the monarchy. Suppression of domestic conspiracies, the defeat of the Spanish Armada, and increasing commercial wealth enlarged both the prestige and power of the Queen. At the national level, Elizabeth controlled all governmental branches by direct or indirect means. County (shire) governments were administered through royally appointed sheriffs and justices of the peace who were responsible to the monarch. The parish, or township, governmental level operated largely through custom, but even at this lowest administrative level in the realm the Queen was a symbol of respect.

The early years of Stuart rule reduced such English pride in their monarchy. Rejecting the Tudor principle of rule through law, James I (1603–1625) and Charles I (1625–1649) adopted the Divine Right concept of government. Its arbitrary application produced corruption, mismanagement, scandal and, more importantly, distrust from growing numbers of Englishmen. Demands for more taxes caused Parliamentary protests, and dispensing of royal monopolies to privileged merchants provoked opposition. One Puritan reflected the ominous mood in 1622 by writing of "the sense of the present evill tymes and the feare of worse." In 1629 King Charles dismissed Parliament, thereby starting a 12-year period of dictatorial rule which led to both increased emigration and a destructive Civil War.

The economic phases of English life on the eve of American colonization showed dislocation as well as expansion. In the countryside, land enclosures designed for more profitable farming drove many tenant farmers as well as the smaller yeomen farmers from their lands. Those who moved to the congested cities found that periodic business depressions often lessened the availability of work even for the existing urban labor force. On the other hand, merchant and banking entrepreneurs were able to reap great profits through individual or joint-stock commercial ventures. Some of the more-affluent bourgeoisie used their prodigious profits in part to gain entrance into the gentry class, while others used their capital to promote a convenient marriage for a daughter or to bestow an education on a talented son.

Religion was a prime consideration for most inhabitants, and it was this feature of English life that was one of the most important aspects of the transmission of culture to America. In 1534, King Henry VIII's Act of Supremacy had severed the nation's long-standing ties with Roman Catholicism. Henry had proceeded to establish a new hierarchical church structure, retaining much Catholic dogma but making the monarch rather than the pope its spiritual leader. This, "popeless though not yet Protestant," Church of England pursued an erratic course following King Henry's death. Under Edward VI (1547–1553) the established church moved further toward a Protestant base, while under Edward's successor, Mary I (1553–1558), it reverted to a Catholic orientation. Elizabeth had ascended to the throne desirous of ending this divisive religious friction. The Thirty-Nine Articles (1571), plus the various Acts of Supremacy and Uniformity and Book of Common Prayer adopted during her reign, finally succeeded in laying a hierarchical, but nevertheless Protestant, basis beneath the Episcopal (Anglican) Church.

The Elizabethan religious settlement did not bring theological harmony or unanimity. A minority of persecuted Roman Catholics refused to accept the Episcopal Church hierarchy and its compromises in religious doctrine. From the opposite standpoint, a significant faction within the Church of England regarded the religious settlement as incomplete and too absolutistic. The group called "Puritans" held varying views on specific policies, yet almost all of them agreed that the Episcopal Church must purge itself of its vestiges of Roman Catholicism and adopt a less-centralized form of church polity. Imbued with theological doctrines from St. Augustine to John Calvin, English Puritans sought to restore a pure, moralistic church on a scriptural basis. In addition to the belief in a predestined elect, they also deemed it essential that each church hold the power to discipline its own members and to expel the corrupt, including even their own pastors.

English Puritans initially had attempted to attain their ends through pamphlets and Parliamentary petitions, but Queen Elizabeth proved unwilling to yield any royal power in spiritual matters. Most Puritans nevertheless continued to seek reforms from within the established church. However, a more radical minority known as Brownists or Separatists concluded that it was sinful to remain within a church that lacked power to discipline itself. During the last decades of Elizabeth's reign groups of these "Separatist" Puritans founded their own independent churches under a system of church polity destined to exemplify New England's Congregationalism.

Theological controversies magnified and coalesced following Queen Elizabeth's death. Persecution of Roman Catholics and dissenting Separatists increased during the reign of James I. Many of the latter group departed for Holland where the Leyden Separatist congregation afterward migrated to New England as the Pilgrim fathers. Nonseparating Puritans, who had hoped that James I from Presbyterian Scotland might be sympathetic to their reformist sentiments, soon learned that the new ruler had no intention of surrendering any of his considerable powers over the monarchically centered Episcopal church. King James rejected the appeals of nonseparating Puritans to reform alleged corruption within the church heirarchy. He also rejected petitions for the toleration of Puritan dominated congregations within the established church and threatened to drive all nonconforming recusants from the land. After the accession of Charles I in 1625, the persecutions became increasingly vexatious. Besides forbidding any innovations in church doctrine or discipline, Charles appointed William Laud Bishop of London in 1628 with broad authority to enforce religious conformity. Puritans, deeply concerned about God's wrath, were thereby faced with two choices. They could conform to an established order which they considered corrupt or, with divine guidance, they could seek a new location to worship in purity. Not surprisingly, many devout Puritans turned to emigration to a New World refuge.

Education in England: 1580–1630

Compared with her continental neighbors, England, by the reign of Charles I, had achieved a noticeably high cultural and intellectual level. It was an age of literary greats—Francis

Bacon, Christopher Marlowe, Ben Jonson, and William Shakespeare. Printing presses published diverse works whose topics varied from popular religious tracts to profane love ballads. The large number of booksellers in urban communities as well as a multitude of public and private libraries were also manifestations of the Englishman's strong penchant for reading. Another indication of this intellectual vitality was a high literacy level; in 1640 it was estimated that the male literacy rate in London was above 50 percent, and in the counties approximately one-third of the men could read. Under such circumstances, the existence of an extensive educational system in England at this time was not surprising.

The precepts encompassing this English educational system were generally identical with those prevailing throughout Western Europe. The belief that social class status and parental desires were the chief determinants of educational attainment were common both on the continent and within England. English families also assumed the principal role in informal vocational education, and maintained the precept that all forms of education must be socially useful. Expanded church participation in learning, which came about as a result of the Reformation, was especially apparent in England where clergymen gave increasing emphasis to more religiously oriented schools for children. Puritan ministers, in particular, emphasized such religious education. Probably the most common similarity between England and the continent, however, was manifested in the indirect role of the state in formal education. As in most Western European states, the English government praised learning and enacted sundry laws for chartering, regulating, or supervising schools, but their general maintenance and support was left almost entirely to private benefactors.

In informal education, the principal event in England at this time occurred in the formalization of its long existant apprenticeship practices. The background causes for this development lay not only in the problem of a rapidly expanding pauper class, but also in the prevalent concept that a harmonious

society must maintain useful callings (occupations) for each
of its members. In 1562 Parliament had passed the Statute of
Artificers that provided an initial basis for support and care
of pauper or indigent children through a program of mandatory apprenticeship. This act was followed by further legislation, reaching a climax in the Poor Laws of 1597 and 1601.
These laws established parish overseers for the poor who, along
with parish churchwardens, were to levy poor rates for the
welfare of the needy, provide labor for employable paupers,
and apprentice the indigent and orphan children of the parish.
The following provisions of the 1601 Poor Law proved especially meaningful in the initial colonial educational legislation:

*Be it enacted by the authority of this present parliament,
that the church-wardens of every parish, and four, three or two
substantial householders there, as shall be thought meet, having respect to the proportion and greatness of the same parish
and parishes, to be nominated yearly in Easter week, or within
one month after Easter, under the hand and seal of two or
more justices of the peace in the same county, whereof one to
be of the quorum, dwelling in or near the same parish or division where the same parish doth lie, shall be called overseers
of the poor of the same parish: and they, or the greater part of
them, shall take order from time to time, by and with the consent of two or more such justices of the peace as is aforesaid,
for setting to work the children of all such whose parents shall
not by the said church-wardens and overseers, or the greater
part of them, be thought able to keep and maintain their children; and also for setting to work all such persons, married or
unmarried, having no means to maintain them, and use no ordi-
nary and daily trade of life to get their living by; and also to
raise weekly or otherwise (by taxation of every inhabitant, par-
son, vicar and other, and of every occupier of lands, houses,
tithes impropriate, propriations of tithes, coal-miners, of sale-
able underwoods in the said parish, in such competent sum and
sums of money as they shall think fit) a convenient stock of*

flax, hemp, wool, thread, iron and other necessare ware and stuff, to set the poor on work; and also competent sums of money for and toward the necessary relief of the lame, impotent, old, blind, and such other among them, being poor and not able to work, and also for the putting out of such children to be apprentices, to be gathered out of the same parish, according to the ability of the same parish, and to do and execute all other things as well for the disposing of the said stock as otherwise concerning the premises, as to them shall seem convenient:

At the onset of English emigration to America, the main features of this state-sponsored apprenticeship system had been widely established. Generally, orphaned or illegitimate children, and those whose parents were considered paupers were apprenticed from ages 5 to 8, to tradesmen or farmers. Their normal length of service was limited by the 1601 Poor Law to age 25 for males and either 21 or the date of marriage for females. The period of service did vary, however, in some parts of the kingdom. While agreements were commonly made requiring the master to provide humane treatment and basic instruction in a trade or occupation, instances of apprentices being maltreated or denied vocational training did exist. In such cases the constables had a right to intervene, and justices were known to abrogate apprenticeships. Conversely, there were enlightened masters who did provide intellectual training. Although the nature of the education an apprentice received was limited by his contract, some masters voluntarily furnished their charges with instruction in reading, writing, and even arithmetic. As for its major purpose, the English apprenticeship system did not approach a solution to the nation's serious economic ills. Yet, despite its obvious shortcomings, the main features of this apprenticeship system were to receive a ready acceptance within England's first colonial settlements.

The growth of formal educational facilities at the elementary and secondary levels in England originated during the latter

part of the sixteenth century. The expansion of formal elementary instruction was most apparent in the founding of large
numbers of parish petty schools or "petties" where boys, and
often girls, were taught reading, writing, religious doctrine, and
sometimes basic arithmetic. Previously, instruction in these
rudimentary fields had been achieved primarily through the
regular monastic orders or in so called "dame schools" conducted by women teaching the alphabet. But the English Reformation had broken up the Catholic monastic orders and the
dame schools proved inadequate at handling the total teaching
burdens. The new model petty schools thus emerged to satisfy
Protestant concerns for a fundamental, orthodox religious education for the children of a community.

Petty schools were located in cities and towns and they were
especially prevalent in rural parishes during the early seventeenth century. Many were in operation on a yearly basis;
others were in session only during specific months of the year,
and in urban centers they were often held in conjunction with
a Latin grammar school. Almost all petty schools were maintained through private benefactors; rarely was any public
taxation used. The benefactions primarily came in the form of
land grants, although individuals were known to endow schools
with cash gifts, property, or livestock. As a result of these bequests, which were especially abundant under the early Stuarts,
many English communities were demonstrating a greater concern over the operation of their petty schools. This concern
was reflected in the supervision that both community and
church officials exercised over items such as textbook selection
and teacher employment. Despite this local surveillance, however, the petties remained essentially private venture schools.
England would have to wait until the late nineteenth century
before securing a true, compulsory, publicly maintained elementary school system.

Children normally entered these elementary level petty
schools from ages five to seven, after learning the alphabet at
home or in a dame school. For the most part, family social

status determined whether or not a child entered one of these fee-paying institutions. There were cases, of course, of poor or apprenticed children gaining admittance without charge, and in some larger communities separate "free schools" were established for poor children. Some petties were held within an individual school building, but they were often located in the master's home or in the parish church. Regardless of its actual site, the school curriculum was dominated by sectarianism. The child learned reading, writing, and basic arithmetic within the doctrinaire concepts of the established church. This factor was readily apparent in the primers and other textbooks used to instruct these young children. Regular and repeated instruction in the approved catechism was another sign of such tutelage. The theologically conscious English society overwhelmingly endorsed this religious indoctrination. Indeed, it was assumed that upon completion of a youth's two or three years training in the petty school, he had attained a firm foundation of spiritual orthodoxy.

A further distinctive feature of the parish schools was the improved quality of the teachers they employed. Although one early Elizabethan statute (1563) had required that prospective teachers be licensed by the diocese bishop, many unlicensed incompetent and even immoral teachers continued to plague the petty schools. Shortly after the accession of James I, however, a concerned Parliament requested bishops to examine the personal and professional qualifications of all schoolmasters within their diocese and to remove all those found unfit. This movement toward improved teacher supervision in England was paralleled by the increased availability of more adequately trained schoolmasters. In fact, it was not unusual during the early seventeenth century to find petty schoolmasters who had attended, although had not completed, studies at one of the English universities. A general improvement in salaries also enhanced the interest in elementary level teaching. Extra remuneration was often available through private tutoring. Some teachers might have complained about their own inferior status in the community by 1630, but at this time both the English elementary schools and their schoolmasters were undoubtedly among the finest in all Europe.

Secondary education in England at this time was distinguished by the town Latin grammar schools. These institutions were distinct from such famed "public" schools as Winchester and Eton whose origins often reached back to the Middle Ages. Many of these "public" schools were originally established to train indigent scholars for the Church but, by the early Stuart period, they had become highly endowed private boarding schools for the sons of the upper classes. Similarly, the town Latin school catered primarily to the upper classes, exclusive of the landed aristocracy, but unlike the more prestigious public schools, the grammar school was a relatively recent vintage. The prototype had emerged from the Latin grammar school founded by Dean John Colet at St. Pauls in London in 1510. It was this model which was generally followed during the educational revival that followed the English Reformation, and by the reign of James I there were few towns of over two thousand inhabitants that lacked such a school.

Boys usually entered these grammar schools at ages seven or eight, following a thorough grounding in English. The curriculum was directed principally toward enabling students to read, write, and speak Latin, although many schools also taught Greek and a few even offered Hebrew. The process of mastering the Roman tongue was lengthy and repetitious; monotonous grammatical rules and a multitude of Latin equivalents for English words were first put to memory; afterwards boys were required to translate innumerable passages from Latin to English, then back to Latin, and finally, the students were put to the repetitious task of composing and reciting Latin declamations. Often competitions between students were used to encourage competence in rhetoric.

Noted classical authors such as Cicero, Horace, Vergil, and Ovid were consulted during this program more for their utilitarian than their literary or intrinsic value. Since most grammar schools enjoined the students to converse constantly in Latin, those who completed the normal six-year program displayed an understandable proficiency in the language.

The Latin grammar school itself was conducted in an austere, formal, and stringent manner. The schoolhouse was usually a small, ascetic structure, holding an average of 50 boys. It was open on a year-round basis with sessions held from early in the morning until late afternoon. Discipline was generally quite strict although sympathetic schoolmasters were not unknown, and many teachers were university graduates. Mixed with the school's intellectual and personal discipline was a rigid religious training marked by recitation of prayers, catechisms, and translations of the Latin New Testament. Students were usually required to attend the parish church on Sundays. Some grammar schools offered a diversion on certain afternoons with instructions in arithmetic, but none of them stressed physical education as part of the boy's training. Bodily exercise was reserved for holidays and after-school hours. This classical-religious foundation was to remain for many years the main hallmark of an English grammar school education.

Aside from such observable, formalized instruction, the town grammar school also provided a basis for the limited social mingling of the sons of privileged Englishmen. A few so-called "free" grammar schools did exist, and a poor boy might have been admitted without charge to a regular grammar school. Most of these tuition institutions, however, were available only to the middle classes and the landed gentry. There, the sons of country squires mixed with the sons of parsons, yeomen farmers, merchants, and professional men. The friendships formed often lasted a lifetime and served to make the grammar school a seasoning ground for many of the nation's future leaders.

English higher education at this time referred to Oxford or Cambridge. Both universities had a long, illustrious history, and by the reign of Charles I their combined student enrollment had reached almost 6,000. Less than 3 percent of the grammar-school matriculants—all from privileged classes—

moved on to higher education, but the university rolls were augmented by the sons of landed aristocrats who usually were prepared by private tutors. Each university was nominally headed by a nonresident chancellor—usually a prominent nobleman—and a vice-chancellor, elected from among the faculty members. In actuality, however, the principal administrative units were the largely autonomous residential colleges of these two institutions. By 1624, Oxford contained 18 such colleges and Cambridge 16, each directed by a provost, rector, president, or master who was subordinated by senior and junior fellows or tutors. The colleges were able to administer almost all their own affairs and, with Parliament's assistance, they received a munificent income from their extensive land endowments.

It was within the confines of each residential college that the students obtained their higher education. Freshmen at Oxford and Cambridge normally entered one of these colleges from ages 14 to 20, although the average age was about 16. Once enrolled, they remained under the careful tutelage of the college fellows or tutors throughout their course of study. Disciplinary action, including expulsion, was generally administered by the director of the college.

The undergraduate curriculum was still primarily based on the medieval university pattern with the accent on rhetoric and logic. Young students preparing their theses, declamations, or public disputations were given a preliminary grounding in Cicero, Quintilian, and Aristotle. They practiced under the scrutiny of individual tutors. The completed works in either Latin or Greek were always given a careful, critical review by the college faculty, and the final senior thesis defense ordinarily attracted large audiences from within and outside the university. Despite a few recent intellectual innovations, such as the more simplistic Ramist approach to theological studies, the bastions of English higher education underwent only a minimum of change during this period.

The university bachelor's degree in England continued to remain the accepted gateway to a favored career. Higher degrees were awarded in the fields of law, medicine, music, and theology, but students were able to enter any of these professions with merely their undergraduate training completed. Young men who had mastered their didactic studies were regarded as well rounded, poised, and intelligent gentlemen, capable of filling a myriad of privileged positions in society. This concept of a well-rounded gentlemen was considered valid for the landed gentry, wealthy merchants, and government officials as well as for those who filled the professional ranks. The belief that colleges trained men to serve church, state, and society would extend far beyond this seventeenth-century British foundation.

For young English girls, a university education was completely impossible. In fact, their limited educational opportunities were a direct reflection of their subordinate status within society. Richard Mulcaster, a prominent schoolmaster, had openly urged that young girls be allowed to share in elementary learning, but it was principally through the Reformation's emphasis on universal literacy that girls were given at least a "tolerated" position in most of the petty schools. Even though more girls had entered the endowed petties in the early seventeenth century, they were often limited in the amount or the type of training they received compared to their male counterparts. In addition, they were usually prohibited from remaining in the school beyond the age of nine, a fact reflected in the poor handwriting and spelling of most Englishwomen. Some private schools for women were founded in urban centers. In these schools, which were limited primarily to daughters of the wealthy, girls studied such "refined" subjects as French, sewing, dancing, and singing. The opportunities for tutorial education were similarly restricted. Britons as yet held little belief in either the social or educational equalization of the sexes.

These, then, were the main features of English education at the onset of American colonization. Contrary to the statements of many earlier educational historians, England did maintain a surprisingly high educational level at this time. Professor Carl

Bridenbaugh has recently estimated that there was "one public secondary school for every 5,687 persons in the realm" and the proportion of the population enrolled in the universities was said to be far greater than at any time until the early nineteenth century. The relatively high level of literacy was additional evidence of the achievements of formal schooling. There were, of course, many drawbacks in such a class-oriented, sectarian dominated educational system, but most Englishmen accepted its main principles. When they migrated to America during the seventeenth century, the colonists naturally sought to reproduce many of the familiar learning patterns of their homeland. The end results produced variances and adjustments to distinctive New World conditions, yet the attempt itself to transplant the educational models of their former culture was to be a characteristic common among English immigrants to the New England, the southern, and the middle colonies of British North America.

education in seventeenth- century new england

the first New England colonists transplanted much of the heritage from Old England to their early settlements but, even more importantly, they carried with them the significant feature of dissent. It was dissent against wickedness from which religious discontentment became the primary propelling force behind their exodus from England. In one way or another, most of these early colonists considered their former homeland as evil, corrupt, and doomed. Therefore, when these first pioneers founded their New England settlements, English institutions were often altered or subordinated in their attempts to establish utopian religious societies. Neither harmony nor religious perfections, however, were achieved in their original "holy commonwealths." The persistence of this characteristic of dissent was clearly revealed among the numerous irreconcilables who discontentedly left Massachusetts Bay to found their own versions of Utopian communities in Connecticut or Rhode Island. Yet despite such ever-present bickerings, jealousies, and schisms, the various seventeenth century New England colonies instituted political, religious, and social precepts which were advanced well beyond those of their English homeland.

The distinctiveness of this region was especially apparent

in its early educational patterns. It will be noted that historians still differ over some of the aspects as well as the historical meaning of the educational systems functioning by the beginning of the eighteenth century. Nevertheless, the advanced attitudes shown toward education, plus the remarkable learning achievements made by most of the people of this frontier region, still remains testimony to the progressive reputation of early New England.

The Seventeenth-Century New England Colonies

The first permanent settlement began at Plymouth Colony in December 1620. The nucleus of the courageous band of colonists who survived the rigors of the initial winter consisted of a group of Separatist Puritans, subsequently known as the Pilgrims. Faced with increased harassment from the established order of King James I, these Pilgrims had originally sought religious refuge in Holland, but afterward they secured a commercial arrangement in England that allowed them to embark on the *Mayflower* for the New World. Though relatively few of their co-believers followed them—one historian estimates less than 200 inhabitants in the colony by 1627—this tiny community in effect had prepared much of the groundwork for the oncoming flood of later immigrants. In addition, several Pilgrim concepts regarding representative government, landholding, and church polity were adopted by subsequent New England colonies.

The origins of Massachusetts Bay Colony, Plymouth's prestigious neighbor, lay among the nonseparating Puritans of England. In contrast to the Separatist groups, the Puritans had remained within the Church of England, although still regarding it as a corrupt institution. Their hopes of reforming this established church had grown exceedingly remote by the reign of Charles I and, as mentioned in the previous chapter, increased restrictions by this monarch, plus the fear of God's approaching punishment on England, caused many of these Puritans to turn toward the New World. By 1629 the way was legally opened for migration through their control of the Massachusetts Bay Company, a chartered commercial body with self-governing rights. Puritans seized this opportunity for migration; they voted to transfer the company charter along with its governing rights to America; they prepared a number of provisioned ships for departure; and in 1630 over 1000 of them led by John Winthrop began the "Great Migration" to New England.

Massachusetts Bay Commonwealth became the focal point of this Great Migration that saw almost 20,000 immigrants settle in New England by its close in 1640. The vast majority of these new arrivals resided initially in Massachusetts Bay where Governor Winthrop had converted the company administration into a self-governing commonwealth. This secular government was at first a limited oligarchy; it did not become representative for over a decade after its beginnings in 1631. Even then, suffrage was restricted to a minority of full church members. Church and state were closely connected within the colony, and, as for church government, the Massachusetts settlers used their settlement in the New World to erect independent meetinghouses where they might practice their version of pure religion. Edmund S. Morgan pointed out that during the years of the Great Migration, the Puritans, despite "previous protestations of loyalty to the Episcopal Church," did not "scruple to construct churches closely resembling the Separatist ones at Plymouth." In these and other institutions, the Bay Commonwealth set the dominant patterns for the entire region.

Subsequent New England colonies developed from this Massachusetts base. In 1636 Roger Williams, banished from Massachusetts for his divergent theological and secular views, founded the first Rhode Island settlement at Providence. Later communities in this small colony were established by Anne Hutchinson, William Coddington, and Samuel Gorton, whose distinctly unorthodox opinions proved equally unwelcome in the Bay Commonwealth. The Reverend Thomas Hooker, who directed the initial settlement of Connecticut, was not expelled from Massachusetts, but part of the reason for his exodus stemmed from his liberal theological beliefs. On the other hand, the Reverend John Davenport and Theophilus Eaton departed from Boston to found the first New Haven Colony settlements because their theological views were more conservative than those of the Bay Commonwealth churches. In fact, during its existence New Haven became the closest colonial approximation to a genuine theocracy in New England. The territories of New Hampshire and Maine were originally granted to English proprietors, yet here also most of the initial settlements were founded and controlled from Massachusetts.

The population of the New England colonies increased during the seventeenth century despite unsettling political events in England and the ravages of King Philip's War (1675–1676). Part of the factors behind this growth lay in a high birth rate and a successful economic diversity. By 1700 the number of inhabitants in New England had superseded that of those colonists living in other sections of British North America. The best population estimates of English colonies at the beginning of the eighteenth century listed 130,000 settlers in New England— 80,000 of whom lived in Massachusetts Bay.

By the end of the seventeenth century, the principal administrative features of the New England colonies were laid down for the inhabitants. In 1684 Massachusetts Bay had its charter revoked by the English government, and seven years later a new charter transformed it into a royal colony with Plymouth Colony incorporated into its bounds. New Hampshire was previously separated as a distinct royal colony in 1680, but the Maine settlements remained a part of Massachusetts until the early nineteenth century. New Haven Colony was formally annexed to Connecticut during the 1660s although Charles II bestowed a liberal charter with broad self-governing powers upon the enlarged colony. Finally, in 1663, the diminutive Rhode Island Colony was also granted a liberal charter by the same monarch. Relatively few changes disturbed the overall administrative situation in New England until the American Revolution.

Economic and Social Life in Seventeenth-Century New England

The primary features of daily life in early New England revolved around the town form of settlement. Several factors influenced the emergence of this type of community living. The generally poor topography and soil of the region lent itself primarily to small, subsistence farming. The fact that emigration to the area was made on a family rather than an individual basis was reflected in the governmental tendency to grant land to specific groups rather than to individuals. The desire to maintain the Puritan ideal of a prevailing religious orthodoxy in the wilderness was still another element behind the move to a more compact form of settlement. In short, it was almost inevitable that the town became such an all-encompassing entity on the landscape.

In their geographical composition, towns followed similar models throughout the region. Usually the legislature of a particular New England colony would bestow a land grant of 25 to 40 square miles to a specific group of freemen who had petitioned it to establish a new town within the colony. Afterward, these freemen would carefully lay out their town plan. Somewhere near the center of the land grant a rectangular lot was set off as the town common and a main road was constructed around it. A meetinghouse was then built on one of the lots facing the common while other lots were reserved for the parsonage, residence of the original proprietors and, in several instances, for the town school. Every freeman was apportioned a strip of land outside the village for his own cultivation. Other adjoining lands were used for common pasturage or common woodland. Any lands that remained unoccupied were kept by the town freemen for subsequent distribution to qualified newcomers.

From within this basic geographical structure, the town developed its most significant political, religious, and social institutions. The popular town meeting emerged as an effective agency of local self-government. Here the town elected its delegates to the colony legislature, chose their selectmen and other town officials, and appointed committees to handle special matters of local concern such as education. In most cases, eligibility for these positions was limited to prominent freemen. While the town meeting was not therefore a democratic institution, those individuals chosen for its offices were at least obligated to comply with the popular wishes of the inhabitants. At the same time the town was expected to set harmonious ethical, religious, and social standards for its inhabitants. Richard Bushman has aptly described the New England town as "a world within itself," in which "family life was fostered, participation in public worship encouraged and the social hierarchy sustained." Under such circumstances education could not escape its all-pervading ascendancy.

The influence of the town was also evident in the economic development of early New England. Around the tightly knit coastal and inland communities the predominant occupations of farming and fishing developed initially. In agriculture especially, success depended on a cooperative communal effort against the wilderness barrier. Towns provided the requisite supervision that saw the growing and merchandising of corn, wheat, beef, and other items of rural husbandry. Even in the prominent work of fishing, coastal communities as a unit furnished much of the support for its growth. A smaller, but still-profitable trade in wood products came largely from the communal woodlands. Although a lesser traffic in furs was a more individualistic operation, the marketing of the pelts was accomplished through town merchants.

During the final decades of the seventeenth century, a re-markable economic expansion was taking place in the region. Indeed, by 1700 Boston with less than 10,000 inhabitants was said to be the third-busiest port in the British Empire. Much of this development was due to the expansion of commerce to more distant markets such as the West Indies and Africa. Though farming and fishing continued to provide the principal employment for most New Englanders, their prominence was being overtaken by the rapidly burgeoning commercial expan-sion. This growth in trade even sparked some small fledgling industries. The full effects of these economic changes were real-ized during the eighteenth century, but by 1700 their effect in areas such as social structure had become apparent.

A social order did emerge in seventeenth-century New Eng-land, but it was not an exact replica of England's social hier-archy. Much of the cause behind this development lay among the original settlers whom the Reverend William Stoughton called "the finest grain in England." While the families that com-prised the bulk of the original immigrants came from most levels of English society, the great landed nobles, and the im-poverished poor were missing from their ranks. The geograph-ical features of the closely knit town settlements was still another factor that prevented the emergence of an English-styled landed aristocracy within the region. Lastly, the necessity for cooperation against a threatening wilderness helped lessen class distinctions—especially on the frontier.

Despite these dissimilarities from Old World features, New England had developed its own social class deliniations by the close of the seventeenth century. Initially, the top layer of this social hierarchy consisted of ministers and prominent magistrates. During the latter half of the century affluent mer-chants also moved into this select group. The next societal level consisted of artisans, tradesmen, and less-prosperous farmers. Below them were the indentured servants and unskilled la-borers. At the extreme (although narrow) base of the social scale were the Indians and Negro slaves. All levels of this societal structure were maintained through efforts of both the civil and the religious establishment.

Religion in New England

The dominant factor in the founding of New England was religion, and its precepts became the predominant concern of almost all its inhabitants during this period. In the forefront of this religious zeal were the Puritans whose theological tenets formed the basis for the established churches in three of the region's four colonies. Even in Rhode Island, where church and state were separate, the first Baptist churches were influenced by Puritan religious doctrine.

In order to understand its vast influence, Puritanism must be first considered as a way of life. Puritans believed in the Calvinist concept of an all-knowing and all-powerful God whose divine precepts were revealed to a dependent mankind through the Scriptures. It was therefore incumbent on those who truly believed in God not only to follow unquestioningly his divinely ordained will, but also to glorify Him in their every action. Thus Puritans, both as individuals and as a group, strove to lead a "smooth, honest, civil life." While this did not mean that they were enjoined to live under austere circumstances, it was nevertheless incumbent upon them to avoid the moral evils and impiety so prevalent in temporal society. They believed that failure to avoid such pitfalls would assuredly bring God's wrath upon all society as well as on the responsible individuals.

The Puritans did not believe, however, that all who scrupulously followed God's will and led an upright life were automatically marked for salvation. By their Calvinist theology, they regarded man as predestined before birth to salvation or to everlasting torment. Outward exhibitions of exemplary social conduct were merely indications but not absolute proof that an individual was among the elect who had achieved God's saving grace. Those who self assuredly proclaimed that good behavior and good works, rather than inner faith, were sufficient to obtain salvation were usually regarded as "unsanctified schismatics." Nevertheless, Puritans did believe that good social conduct was at least positive evidence that an individual might have saving faith, and so they intensified their personal efforts to achieve virtue and to avoid immorality. Their lives, therefore, were constantly filled with inner self-examination and self-reproach in which they endeavored to bring their personal lives in line with the divine precepts of the Bible.

The focal points for such beliefs as well as the center of the Puritan "visionary" communities rested in the meetinghouses (churches) of the individual towns. It was previously noted that the Puritans used their migration to break with England's established Episcopal order and to establish a more autonomous church structure. Under this system Puritan ministers or teaching elders held only limited power in their own meetinghouses. The principal power was held by the church members who appointed and removed their individual pastors. Full church membership, however, was not a simple matter; in fact it required visible evidence of saving faith, including competence in the Scriptures. The majority of inhabitants who failed to obtain church membership were nevertheless enjoined to attend regular religious worship services. Also, whether one was a church member or a nonchurch member, all inhabitants of the community were obligated to conform to the scripturally based moral code expounded from the pulpit of the meetinghouse.

The institutions of secular government in Puritan settlements were closely aligned to the ecclesiastical order. Puritans believed that temporal governments existed for the primary function of enforcing obedience to God and His holy commandments. Since the power of the churches over their nonmember majority was quite minimal, the decisive power of the state was invoked to achieve this idealistic moral order. In addition, since Puritans considered it dangerous for their pastors to exercise civil authority, they expected that both ministers and magistrates would work together in their compliance with God's will. Governments were expected to collect taxes for minister's salaries and to enforce church decisions while the church, for its part, was to proclaim the supremacy and sanctity of the state. Massachusett's first legal code, the 1639 Laws and Liberties of Massachusetts was, in fact, based upon both English Common Law and the Scriptures. While this church-state cooperation to achieve a virtuous society reached its fullest expression within individual towns, it was apparent on a broader basis in ordinances such as the Cambridge Platform (1648), the ecclesiastical constitution for most seventeenth-century Puritan congregations.

Puritan concepts concerning democracy and religious toleration coincided with the views on church and state. Despite the harassment they had received in the Episcopal homeland, they held no intentions of establishing democratic communities open to all religious creeds. To orthodox Puritans, governments that practiced civil democracy and complete religious freedom were actually anarchistic societies. Puritan ministers John Cotton and Nathaniel Ward supported such sentiments. Cotton stated, "If the people be governors who shall be governed" while Ward wrote that religious toleration was certainly the handiwork of Satan. In this desire to maintain a strict orthodoxy within their communities, Puritans therefore refused to allow room for any serious dissension. Until 1691, the prestigious Massachusetts Bay Colony denied the suffrage to non-church members; and their banishment of dissidents such as Roger Williams exemplified their demand for orthodoxy.

Economic and social life in seventeenth-century New England was also influenced by Puritanism. In the former case, it centered around the concept of the "calling." The Puritans believed that God called every man to serve him by serving society in some useful, productive occupation. All such worldly callings or occupations were said to be equal in God's sight, but it was incumbent upon each individual to be reasonably certain that he held the necessary qualifications to embark upon this beneficial work. Once an individual had begun his particular calling, it then was expected that he would demonstrate virtuous attributes such as diligence and thrift.

Similarly, this belief in divine determination led Puritans to justify their particular social heirarchy. Although they presumed that God regarded all mankind as equally corrupted by original sin, this was not understood to mean that all men were equal in temporal relations with each other. Thus, beginning at the family level, the Puritans established a system of societal subordination—viz., parents over children, husband over wife, masters over servants. It was a subordination which continually stressed rank and deference to one's superiors, and by the close of the seventeenth century, its effects were still apparent in all societal features including education.

Finally, Puritanism and its relationship to learning must be noted before undertaking a survey of the educational strivings and achievements of those who followed its doctrines. As an intellectual creed Puritans placed a heavy stress on knowledge that they believed invariably reflected God's omnipotence. In the printed word, especially the classics, they found innumerable examples for their own moral and spiritual guidance. Their sentiments were displaced in the widespread popularity and wide variety of books found in New England. At least 20 booksellers operated shops in Boston between 1669 and 1692, while numerous independent peddlers sold volumes to eager inhabitants in outlying communities. Substantial individual libraries were transported to New England as early as the Great Migration, and a number of collections, such as those of Cotton Mather and John Winthrop Jr., reached into the thousands of volumes. Most of the titles in private and public libraries and in bookshops were religious, but a vast number of diverse secular topics also appeared along with works authored by non-Puritan, non-Protestant, and even non-Christian authors.

Of more immediate relevance to education was the essential role that knowledge played in Puritanism's concept of salvation. Puritans, by their Calvinist orientation, were convinced that saving faith came directly from God to the individual pre-destined elect. Obtaining this saving faith, they believed, was an intellectual as well as a spiritual process, and they were there-fore convinced that without knowledge salvation was impos-sible. For them ignorance, particularly ignorance of the Scrip-tures, was mankind's chief adversary, whereas understanding helped bring men closer to God. Since all children were pre-sumed to have been born in ignorance, it was incumbent on both the family and the community to see that their children were prepared for possible salvation by teaching them the doc-trines and principles of Christianity. Church members were especially obligated by their particular status to educate their children. It was generally felt that a society's failure to promote learning opened the way for evil. From such fundamental be-liefs as these, a remarkable educational system blossomed within the wilderness of seventeenth century New England.

Historical Appraisals of Seventeenth-Century New England Education

Many historians have examined and assessed the educational patterns that existed in early New England. As might be ex-pected, their resultant studies have emerged with varying in-terpretations. Some writers have differed over the underlying purposes of Puritan education; others have argued over the extent of its availability. One of the most basic areas of dis-agreement, however, is in the overall historical appraisal of the Puritan educational system, in effect, New England's only edu-cational system at that time.

The first significant historical assessments of Puritan educa-tion began during the final decades of the nineteenth century. Represented by scholars such as George H. Martin and E. Ben-jamin Andrews, the general consensus was that Puritan New England, led by Massachusetts, established an outstanding, al-most universal system of popular education throughout its early settlements. Martin, in fact, firmly upheld the principle that the first appearance of free public education in America could be traced to the Massachusetts Puritans. Most of Martin's contemporary educational historians reflected this appraisal in their own writings. Publicly supported schools were pictured as common in almost all Puritan settlements; attendance was said to be practically universal at well-administered schools; and illiteracy was alleged to have been largely nonexistent among these early New England colonists. Such elevated assessments continued into the present century.

One of the most noted writers in this century who stressed the pervasive influence of Puritan education was Ellwood Cubberley. Cubberley, who was superintendent of San Francisco public schools and teacher at Stanford University, elaborated his views in his popular work, *Public Education in the United States*. In this book, which was first published in 1919, Cubberley traced the roots of public education in the United States to seventeenth-century New England. He maintained that the Puritans who settled New England "contributed most that was valuable for our future educational development, and established in practice principles which have finally been adopted generally by our different states." In addition, he argued that the Massachusetts Bay School Laws of 1642 and 1647 laid the fundamental basis "for the compulsory education of all children and the compulsory town maintenance of schools." Cubberley's concepts remained predominant among most American educational historians until about the beginning of World War II.

In recent decades, a revisionist approach has appeared, reevaluating the scope of Puritan education. Several contemporary writers have denied Cubberley's assertions that the Massachusetts Bay School Laws represented the foundations upon which our American state public school systems were built. Represented by scholars such as Harvard's Bernard Bailyn and Columbia's Lawrence Cremin, these revisionists have further maintained that the older group of educational historians had failed to place education within its proper historical, religious, intellectual and social perspectives, thereby "misreading modern concepts of public education into the Puritan system." Bailyn, in his book, *Education in the Forming of American Society*, accentuated the fact that most of these earlier historians "failed to notice the essential differentiation between the present and the past." He noted, for example, that "the modern conception of public education, with the very idea of a clean line of separation between private and public, was unknown before the eighteenth century." Along with other contemporary historians Bailyn concluded that Puritan educational patterns were basically imitative of their English cultural heritage and that deviations from these traditions resulted from a basic alteration of social institutions within a New World environment. Lawrence Cremin's prodigious and scholarly volume, *American Education: The Colonial Experience, 1607–1783*, expands on Bailyn's theses by describing this broad and rich English heritage in detail and the extent to which it was transplanted in America.

Regardless of this recent revisionist reinterpretation of the actual influence and meaning of Puritan education, these early New England pioneers undoubtedly made remarkable achievements in learning. Their vigorous emphasis on education was sustained even within the hostile, restrictive conditions of the strange new environment. Perpetuating learning, while at the same time carving out a new civilization, was not an easy task. By 1700, however, Puritans not only had preserved the traditions of classical learning, but their New England colonies could also boast of literacy rates that were often superior to those existing in England. (Suffolk County Massachusetts, during the period of 1681 to 1697, was reputed to have had a literacy rate of 89 and 62 percent for men and women, respectively.) Such noteworthy accomplishments were made within a social order that regarded the establishment of schools available to all children as absolutely essential for the perpetuation of their way of life. It was not surprising, therefore, that Puritans deviated from the English practice of indirect state participation in education, and substituted a direct governmental role in requiring both colonywide mandatory education and school maintenance.

Compulsory Education and
Compulsory School Maintenance Legislation

Initially, the Puritan settlers of Massachusetts Bay had attempted to transplant the more traditional patterns of their English homeland into their early schools. During the 1630s private benefactors were relied upon as the principal source for founding and maintaining schools within the colony. This practice, transferred from England, was illustrated by the private donations used to found institutions such as Boston's Latin Grammar School (1635) and Harvard College (1636). At this early stage in formal learning, the states' role was largely indirect. Aside from reproducing replicas of English apprenticeship statutes for informal education, the Massachusetts General Court did not take immediate steps to require either compulsory education for all children or compulsory maintainence of schools.

Circumstances soon forced the Massachusetts Bay government to deviate from these English practices and to undertake a more direct role in formal educational procedures. Although some men of moderate means had been among the first settlers in the Great Migration, the general absence of wealthy Puritan migrants limited the degree of dependence upon rich benefactors for school support. Unlike England, the Bay Colony wilderness lands were unable to produce a reliable source for educational funding. This absence of surplus wealth and dependable forms of investment was matched by the general inability of many Puritan families to perform their educational functions. Faced with the everpresent rugged environment many Puritan parents and masters were often unable to devote much time to the formal tutoring of their children.

Puritans soon became aware of this inadequacy of the traditional forms of educational support and the decline of the cus-

tomary family role in education. They feared not only a declining family educational role but, even more, the destruction of
the family structure itself. They were also concerned about the
subversion of their basic cultural standards in a society that
lacked adequate learning facilities. Most importantly, these
Biblically oriented Puritans were apprehensive that the absence
of adequate education would mean the collapse of their attempt
to implant pure religious societies in the New World. Their
ministers equated the surrounding wilderness with barbarism,
and unless the community's children received a sound, sectarian education, anarchy was expected to follow. Puritans consequently turned to the state for assistance.

The initial response of the Massachusetts General Court came
in the educational law of 1642. The statute began by condemning "the great neglect of many parents and masters in training
up their children in learning, and labor and other imployments
that may be profitable to the common wealth." It continued by
ordering the selectmen in each town, under penalty of a fine, to
ascertain whether or not parents and masters were following
their obligations to provide "for the calling and employment of
their children." It was also incumbent upon these selectmen to
determine if the children were being taught "to read and understand the principles of religion and the capital laws of this
country." Individuals who refused to allow an examination of
their children could be fined. In addition, if the selectmen dis-
covered any parents or masters remiss in fulfilling their obligations, these local officials, with the consent of any court or
magistrate, could apprentice out those children who had failed
to meet the requirements of this statute. It was then obligatory
for the new master of each deficient child to fulfill all the provisions of the law. A concluding portion of the act required each
selectman to give a brief account of his actions in complying
with its provisions.

Much of the wording of this compulsory education law reflected previous English statutes but, at the same time, took a
significant step beyond previous legislation toward compulsory

education. The obligation on all children to learn a trade or calling in order to prevent an increase in the number of paupers was clearly an echo of the English Poor Law of 1601. This familiar economic interest was given added weight in the colonies by the fact that skilled labor was scarce and wages were consequently higher than in the mother country.

Yet the School Law of 1642 had gone beyond the customary poor relief economic provisions. Unlike the English Poor Law of 1601, the later Massachusetts statute had instituted the unique provisions that parents and masters were responsible for their children's ability to read, understand the basic principles of Puritan beliefs, and know the "capital laws" of the colony. The religious and political motivations of the Puritans thereby were linked directly to the continued security and stability of what they considered their "holy society." In addition, by incorporating Puritan aims into this statute, Massachusetts had taken the first step toward establishing a colony-wide system of compulsory education.

The School Law of 1642 was "to continue for two years," but it was not until 1648 that the statute underwent any alteration. At this time the General Court somewhat more specifically required that children and apprentices learn "some short orthodox" catechism and be prepared to answer questions concerning it. Selectmen were given the responsibility for judging the competence of individual children and apprentices. Besides examining these children in this specific religious requirement, the town selectmen were again ordered to determine if individual youths were taught reading, the capital laws, and were being "brought up in some honest lawful calling, labour, or imployment." Also, as in 1642, the selectmen might, with the assistance of the court or two magistrates, take children or apprentices from families that failed to meet the stipulations of the law and apprentice them to a family that would carry out the provisions of the act. Fines of 20 shillings were levied on negligent parents or masters. Girls who were apprenticed were to serve until they were 18, and boys until they were 21.

Earlier in the twentieth century, the noted historians Charles and Mary Beard described the motives of the School Laws of 1642 and 1648 as simply attempts to exploit the labor of the poor to impose "on all children the creed of the Puritan sect." Recent scholars such as Bernard Bailyn, Lawrence Cremin, and Edmund S. Morgan have shown the erroneous nature of this generalization. Their studies have explained that at the heart of both these educational statutes lay an overwhelming concern for maintaining the primary role of the family in the ordering of society. Puritans certainly believed that the family held vital connections with the economic and religious structures of their settlements. It therefore becomes more obvious that the School Laws of 1642 and 1648 were attempts to avoid a decay in family life by requiring a basic minimum of learning and vocational skills.

With the exception of dissident Rhode Island, the Massachusetts statutes of 1642 and 1648 became models for all other New England colonies during the seventeenth century. The Connecticut Law Code of 1650 included an almost exact restatement of the Bay Colony statute of 1648. New Haven Colony adopted a system of mandatory education in 1655 which made no direct mention of vocational education but which required more academic and sectarian training than the Massachusetts Laws. In 1671 Plymouth Colony enacted its own compulsory educational legislation based largely on the existing Massachusetts laws. Since Maine was part of Massachusetts from 1652 onward, and New Hampshire from 1641 to 1680, the relatively few communities within these regions were also subject to these statutes during a large part of this century.

Legislation requiring the establishment of colonywide standards of compulsory education nevertheless did not establish schools, nor did it order compusory attendance at such schools. Satisfying the provisions of this act was left entirely up to individual parents or masters. While it was assumed that children could be tutored within the home or enrolled in some form of community schooling, circumstances restricted the actuality of obtaining a requisite education in either of these re-spects. In 1642, only a small percentage of Massachusetts towns had established schools, and many parents and masters were simply unable to provide the necessary education by them-selves. As a result, the colony's Puritan leaders again turned hopefully and entreatingly to the state for assistance.

In 1647, the Massachusetts General Court responded once more and departed from traditional English educational pat-terns. This time the legislature enacted the famous "Old Deluder Law," which set the basic patterns for compulsory town schools in New England. The law first of all compelled towns of 50 householders to make provisions for instruction in reading and writing, and it offered possible ways and means of financing such instruction. Secondly, the act stipulated that the few existing towns of at least 100 householders or families must establish a Latin grammar school to prepare boys for Harvard. A concluding provision levied a £5 fine upon negligent communi-ties. The actual wording of the "Old Deluder Law" illustrates its unique position in the history of American education:

It being one chief project of that old deluder, Satan, to keep men from the knowledge of the Scriptures, as in former times by keeping them in an unknown tongue, so in these latter times by persuading from the use of tongues, that so at least the true sense and meaning of the original might be clouded by false glosses of saint-seeming deceivers, that learning may not be buried in the grave of our fathers in the church and common-wealth, the Lord assisting our endeavors.

It is there for ordered that every township in this jurisdic-tion, after the Lord hath increased them (in) number to fifty householders, shall then forthwith appoint one within their town to teach all such children as shall resort to him to write and read, whose wages shall be paid either by the parents or masters of such children, or by the inhabitants in general, by way of supply, as the major part of those that order the pru-dentials [affairs] of the town shall appoint; provided those that send their children be not oppressed by paying much more than they can have them taught for in other towns; and it is further ordered that where any town shall increase to the number of 100 families or householders, they shall set up a grammar school, the master thereof being able to instruct youth so far as they may be fitted for the university, provided that if any town neglect the performance hereof above one year, that every such town shall pay £5 to the next school till they shall perform this order.

The School Law of 1647 was intended to fill not only existing learning deficiencies, but also to insure education, religious orthodoxy, and cultural standards for future generations. This serious concern for posterity was clearly illustrated in the phrase, "that learning may not be buried in the grave of our fathers in church and commonwealth." By 1647 this threat of general illiteracy seemed clearly imminent to Puritans. The General Court had determined that in future, therefore, the obligation to provide the teaching for the young would devolve upon the town rather than upon the parent. It was now expected that the colony's towns would fulfill these obligations principally through the establishment and maintenance of schools. Since it was a "chief project of that old deluder Satan to keep men from the knowledge of the Scriptures" it was expected, moreover, that such schools would focus on reading so that children might obtain a direct understanding of the Bible.

Most other New England colonies followed Massachusetts' leadership in the Old Deluder Law, just as they had its compulsory education statutes. Rhode Island once again proved the most divergent from the Bay Colony model, and its colonial government failed to obligate its towns to establish and maintain schools.

Elsewhere, Connecticut followed Massachusetts' example most closely by adopting the 1647 statute almost verbatim in its legal code of 1650. Although New Haven Colony failed to pass an act requiring towns to establish schools, the Connecticut statute became applicable to New Haven following its absorption into Connecticut. In 1672, the enlarged Connecticut Colony required that a grammar school be established in each of its four counties. The Plymouth Colony legislature in 1658 recommended that its towns hire schoolmasters to teach their children reading and writing. In 1673, Plymouth's General Court reserved £33 annually from its Cape Cod fishery profits to maintain a grammar school, and in 1677, it donated £5 to £10 annually from these profits to towns then maintaining such schools. At the same time the act of 1677 required those towns not maintaining a grammar school to pay £5 annually to the nearest town supporting this type of institution. Maine, as part of Massachusetts, became subject to the provisions of the Old Deluder Law from 1652 onward. Finally, New Hampshire was legally subject to the Massachusetts Law of 1647 until its separation in 1680, but it nevertheless continued the provisions of this statute while a royal colony.

Enforcement of Compulsory Education and Compulsory School Laws

The enactment of compulsory education and compulsory school legislation was one subject; enforcing such legislation was another topic. Some historians have differed significantly in their estimates of how far these school statutes were enforced. For example, the late Charles M. Andrews wrote that these school laws "were more honored in the breach than the observance" and that "even when honestly carried out they produced but slender results." Other historians have declared conversely that these laws were well enforced. One such individual was Marcus Jernegan who cited several examples of parents who were fined for failure to obey the Massachusetts statutes of 1642 and 1648.

It is difficult to make any absolute assessment concerning this issue of enforcement. Naturally, the most adequate means of determining the degree of enforcement would result from a close examination of the town and county court records from seventeenth-century New England colonies. Unfortunately, serious deficiencies prevent such a broad examination. As Samuel Eliot Morison has written, "Town records are fragmentary; of existing county court records only those of Essex County Massachusetts, and ten years of Suffolk have been printed." He also pointed out that reliable population data is lacking "to tell us which towns had over fifty or over one hundred families, making them liable to support common, or both common and grammar schools." Even the figures from which estimates concerning literacy were made cannot be used to determine adequately the acutal execution of school laws.

Some general conclusions however, can be made regarding this relevant question. First, it is apparent that the various educational statutes did not operate with complete effectiveness. Several small frontier settlements and individual parents still found it too difficult to comply with the existing school statutes. Even coastal Essex County, during a 44-year period, had six towns accused and one of them fined for failure to comply with educational laws. The difficulties of compliance persisted, especially from the period of King Philip's War (1675–1676) to the end of the century. By this time a significant number of frontier communities were trying to obtain exemptions from the colony school laws or were being indicted for failure to obey them. Puritan ministers such as Cotton Mather and Thomas Shepard complained of shortcomings in the educational system, and both Connecticut and Massachusetts felt it necessary to raise the fines on communities failing to comply with compulsory school laws. By 1701 the Massachusetts General Court still complained that many towns were failing to enforce the school law of 1647.

At the same time, it is also true that the majority of New England Puritans maintained their strong concern for learning, and most of them continuously strove to provide instruction for their children. Thus a gross exaggeration was made by one early twentieth-century educational historian who claimed that the latter half of the seventeenth century saw an "extreme decadence in educational affairs" that expressed "the opposition of the people to the schools." The majority of Puritan communities during this period did, in fact, attempt to offer some form of schooling. For example, Northampton and Hadley established schools in 1665 and 1666 respectively, shortly after their founding along the frontier. Most parents, masters, and individual communities apparently did agree to fulfill provisions of the school laws after warnings from judicial authorities. Also reflecting this overall educational concern was a general lack of illiteracy. A careful study by Clifford K. Shipton revealed "that throughout the entire colonial period the level of literacy remained amazingly high in spite of the death of the first generation, the demands of frontier life, and of Indian Wars." It seems probable, therefore, that even those Puritan communities that lacked town schools were generally able to provide some form of elementary instruction to satisfy the relevant provisions of the laws of 1642, 1647, and 1648.

A clearer assessment regarding legal enforcement can be made about secondary education in Puritan settlements. Although the claim that Latin Grammar schools were "rare" is exaggerated, it is evident that most communities of over 100 families in both Connecticut and Massachusetts failed to maintain such required secondary schools. A study by Morison found only 11 New England towns supporting grammar schools for "any appreciable length of time in the seventeenth century," and that "only four seem to have had an unbroken existence from the first ten or fifteen years of the colony's existence." More recently, Robert Middlekauff estimated that 25 grammar schools were operating in New England in 1700. Yet, even granting the accuracy of this revised estimate, it is still evident that only a minority of the larger Puritan settlements supported grammar schools.

Finally, it should be noted that despite shortcomings in their actual execution, the very existence of such school laws had set the basis for New England's particular educational system. Much of this system bore the markings of an English or European heritage, but some of it did relate to the unique conditions of the New World environment. A survey of informal and formal learning procedures in seventeenth-century New England illustrates the various characteristics of this remarkable system of education.

Informal Education in Seventeenth-Century New England

In "Old England" as well as in New England informal education centered first of all within the family circle. Both Bernard Bailyn and Lawrence Cremin find, in the family, the principal means through which the colonists adapted to the pressures of their new environment. It was the family group in both regions that gave infants the initial insight into their physical environment and provided their beginning guide to religion and morality. Yet within New England, the family role in informal education became even more distinctive for Puritans. Their ministers described the family as the "root where Church and Commonwealth cometh," and they depended on the family circle to provide the earliest essential moral and religious training. Believing that all children were born both ignorant and prone toward sin, Puritans strove to begin the child's informal education as early as possible. Their concern for their children's salvation broadened parental tasks in informal education. At an early age children were taught a reverence for their parents; they were instructed in good habits and morality; and their fathers were legally bound to instruct them each week in a catechism. Beyond such prime moral and religious duties, it was the household that provided the initial training in what would be the eventual vocational calling of each child.

The principal informal training for a child's vocational calling stemmed from the apprenticeship system. In New England the characteristics of the apprenticeship system had been brought directly from England. Among Puritans however, apprenticeships went beyond a basic need to satisfy their existent labor shortage. They broadened the Old World vocational concept of contractual apprenticeships to include mandatory obligations on the masters to provide instruction in literacy, religious precepts, and civil laws of their community. In short, Puritan economics and education went hand in hand.

All New England colonies were covered by some form of apprenticeship legislation during the seventeenth century. Although Massachusetts enacted general taxation laws in 1634 and in 1638 that were clearly based on the English Poor Law of 1601, it was not until the school law of 1642 was passed that this colony's mandatory apprenticeship requirements were formally spelled out. Subsequent Massachusetts statutes reiterated the masters' obligation to provide requisite education and vocational training—especially for poor or orphaned children. Connecticut and New Haven Colony closely followed the legislative example of Massachusetts regarding apprentices, both before and after their union in 1664. Plymouth Colony's first apprenticeship law was passed in 1641 and was quite similar to the Poor Law of 1601. Subsequent apprenticeship legislation in this colony followed the Massachusetts pattern. Since they were part of Massachusetts, Maine and New Hampshire (up to 1680) were subject to its laws. Even Rhode Island acted in this field when, in 1662, it enacted the apprenticeship provisions of the English Poor Law of 1601 and empowered towns to "put out to service" all children likely to become public charges.

The method and the length of apprenticeships in New England were not dissimilar from prevailing English practices. In both cases all children were generally given some tasks at a very early age. For girls in a Puritan family apprenticeship training for the fundamental calling of housewife began as early as age 6 or 7—while for boys vocational instruction began somewhat later—between ages 10 to 14. Orphans or wards of both sexes were formally apprenticed at as early an age as convenient. The apprenticeships generally terminated for boys at 21 and for girls at 18 or until the time of marriage.

The basic English features of apprenticeship continued into eighteenth century New England. Unlike England however, the Puritan colonies had made their apprenticeships unique by using them as instruments for compelling the education of all youth. Only dissident Rhode Island had failed to place any legislative requirements on the masters to provide a literacy education for their charges. Originally, it had been expected that Puritan masters themselves would fulfill these legal obligations for instruction, but by 1700 most of them had been obligated to rely on established schools to teach their apprentices.

Elementary Education in
Seventeenth-Century New England

Dame schools and tutorial instruction, both imitations of English practices, were the initial methods of elementary instruction instituted in Puritan New England. Parents themselves might teach their children the alphabet, basic reading, spelling, and religious doctrines, or they could send their children to a private "reading" or dame school. These private schools were usually held in a resident's home. In a number of settlements either private venture schools or family tutoring were the principal means used to satisfy existing educational statutes. Boston, for example, observed the Massachusetts educational statutes although no elementary level "public" school was established in the community until 1684. In some towns the private dame schools became semipublicly or publicly maintained community institutions. Reliance on these restricted methods for universal elementary instruction proved impractical, however, and they were soon overshadowed in Puritan New England by numerous public, town, or "writing" schools.

It was this public, town, or writing school as it was sometimes called that became the main hallmark of elementary education during the seventeenth century. While these New England schools bore similarities to the English petty schools, they also had significant differences. Unlike the private venture "petties," the town schools were tax-supported public institutions. Private donations and bequests were often used to found these town schools in New England, but they were supplemented by compulsory or voluntary contributions and public land grants. In addition, while both petty and town schools almost invariably charged fees, New England communities generally assumed the cost for those poor children unable to pay the town school charges. Thus, Watertown, Massachusetts approved the following resolution in 1696 regarding its town school fees: "Voted allso that the Town will pay for such children as these parents are not abell to pay for, the select men Being Judges of that matter." As this resolution indicates, community control over town schools was much broader than that exerted over the English petty school. Finally, the town schools, unlike the "petties," were never maintained exclusively for the benefit of the rich and the orthodox believers but were open to every child in the community.

All New England colonies maintained town schools during the seventeenth century. In Massachusetts, a number of communities such as Charlestown, Salem, Ipswich, Dorchester, and Newbury had established town schools before the Old Deluder Law of 1647 was enacted. The original Bay Colony schools were supported by a variety of methods, but by the close of the century the most common basis was a combination of fees, gifts, and mandatory town rates. One educational historian estimated that in 1700 over one-third of Massachusetts towns— which would then include those in Plymouth and in Maine— were operating town schools. New Hampshire's first town school was established shortly after the settlement of Hampton in 1638, and by the time it separated from Massachusetts, three of its four towns were maintaining such schools. New Haven in 1641 ordered that "a free schoole be sett up in this town" while about the same time Mr. William Andrews was conducting a town school in Hartford. One Connecticut historian estimated that all the river towns in this colony had town

schools by 1665. Dissident Rhode Island even had a few instances of town schools during this century: Barrington kept
its town school operating after its incorporation into Rhode
Island and Bristol, in 1682, had a school supported by a rate
and a three-pence-per-week fee.

The curriculum of town schools was narrow in scope and
religiously oriented. Although it was expected that most children who entered the town schools for one or two years study
had learned to read at home or in a dame school, many town
schoolmasters had to instruct their students in this subject.
After the children were able to read to the master's satisfaction,
he generally began to instruct them in writing. It is recalled
that instruction in both reading and writing were a part of
the colony's required elementary instruction. While in some
cases basic arthmetic or ciphering might also be taught in town
schools, there were so called "writing schools" that specialized
in writing and arithmetic. One such writing school was opened
in Boston in 1684, but these institutions never became as popular as the regular town schools. Arithmetic was not considered
essential to the education of most of the elementary level
students, so that any rudimentary instruction offered was
purely utilitarian and mechanical.

The town meeting was the earliest and most prevalent means
of school control. When the law of 1647 was enacted, it left all
details regarding its implementation to the townspeople themselves. The town meeting therefore was originally empowered
to levy taxes for school support, to select the school site, to
hire the schoolmaster, and to perform other administrative
or supervisory functions. Gradually however, Puritan towns
began to delegate much of their authority to the selectmen. In
1654 a Massachusetts law recommended that the selectmen of
the colony's towns exercise some supervision over the quality
of the teachers employed by the community. As the century
drew to a close, the towns tended to surrender further executive and legislative school authority to the selectmen. Another
Massachusetts statute enacted in 1693 apparently recognized

this development. It required both towns and selectmen to see that schools were maintained, and the selectmen were authorized to levy school taxes, provided that a majority of the townspeople had previously voted to direct them to do so.

One primary concern of Puritan townspeople was the hiring of a qualified schoolmaster. College graduates were naturally among the town's first choice for candidates. Their availability was limited, however, and despite the security offered to them by teaching, most college graduates entered the profession only as a waystation to the pulpit. As a result many towns were forced to choose other, less-qualified persons for administering their schools. In 1697 Malden, Massachusetts employed an elderly, inexperienced ex-seaman as its schoolmaster while Portland (Maine) later used a shoemaker-cordwinder as its teacher. A number of towns, however, were able to hire well-qualified, although not always permanent, schoolmasters. Clifford Shipton points out for example, that only one of Newbury's first 11 schoolmasters was not a college graduate, and that Dedham had 27 teachers in 60 years—all but the first three being fresh from Harvard.

The nature of schoolmaster's salaries was another factor that affected the quality of elementary education during the seventeenth century. Several towns directed their selectmen to hire a teacher at the cheapest possible rate, but the lack of able candidates often made the task difficult unless the selectmen were willing to overlook the background of the candidates. The general scarcity of money presented another problem. Most schoolmasters were obliged to accept a portion of their salary in produce; Maine towns, for example, often paid teachers in lumber or fish. In some instances, housing or the possibility of additional employment was used as an added incentive. In many cases, too, the schoolmaster added to his salary by levying a fee on those students who could afford it. Morison states that the usual fee in the seventeenth century was three pence a week for the elementary level and a penny higher for grammar schools. On the whole, however, elementary schoolmasters in New England were not underpaid, and the prestige they received in some towns was a further reflection of the remarkable educational achievement at this level.

The Latin Grammar School

The most prominent institutions of secondary education in New England at this time were the public grammar schools. Although boys could receive formal training for college through tutoring, ministerial instruction, or in a few instances private grammar schools, it was the public grammar school that emerged as the principal means for both college preparation and a general education. The English Latin grammar school was intended to be the basic model, but very few Puritan towns established a complete replica of the prototype. Also unlike England, the New England public grammar school was completely controlled by the towns and their delegated officials. As Morison wrote: "Not a penny of church money was used for the schools; their support came entirely from secular sources." Community control and support remained a hallmark of these public grammar schools established during the seventeenth century.

The first public grammar school in New England originated in Boston. In 1635 the town meeting recommended that "Philemon Pormont shall be entreated to become schole master for the teaching and nourtering of children," and the following year the wealthier inhabitants met and subscribed funds to maintain a schoolmaster. This beginning of the famed Boston Latin School was matched within a decade by the founding of grammar schools in five other Bay Colony towns. Although the Massachusetts School Law of 1647 required larger communities to maintain a grammar school and instituted fines for noncompliance, it was not until after King Philip's War that a significant increase in the number of these schools occurred within the colony.

New Hampshire as a royal colony reenacted the Old Deluder

Law, but by the century's close, only the town of Portsmouth was conducting a grammar school. Although the Connecticut legislature had adopted the provisions of the Old Deluder Law in 1650, 22 years later it was revised to require only one grammar school in each of the colony's four counties. In 1690, the maintenance of the existing grammar schools at New Haven and Hartford was deemed sufficient to satisfy the colony's legal requirements. In Rhode Island private sources provided the only means of secondary education at this time.

Boys usually entered the grammar schools at ages seven or eight, following reading and writing instruction in their homes, dame schools, or in some cases a town school. The instruction that they received was intended to copy the patterns of the English grammar Schools. After a brief period of repractice in reading. writing and reciting the catechism, the boys were put to the main purpose of their studies—the ability to read, write, and converse in Latin. The first years usually went spent in rote memorization of an "accidence" or beginning Latin grammar, a Latin-English phrasebook, and a vocabulary. The boys were next required to read from the works of famous classical and Renaissance authors such as Cicero, Vergil, Ovid, and Erasmus. At the same time the boys were expected to prepare Latin themes or verses for their schoolmasters' scrutiny. Basic rhetoric and elementary Greek were usually begun during the last year of study, but Hebrew was reserved for higher education. If arithmetic was offered, it was normally taught on the same elemental basis as in the town schools. After about seven years of such secondary, classically oriented training it was expected that most of the graduates were prepared for college.

Not all these New England secondary schools offered this curriculum and most elementary and secondary schools were conducted in a more austere environment than in the English schools. The strict Puritan religious beliefs were reflected in a severe disciplinary code inherited from England. Cotton Mather's epigram, "Better whipped than damned" was put into practice by solemn schoolmasters with their everpresent birch rods. Saturday afternoons were set aside for rigorous religious indoctrination.

Schoolbuildings themselves reflected the stringent instruction. When they existed as structures separate from meetinghouses or private homes, the early schoolbuildings were usually crude, austere edifices. Town schools were especially small; the average room dimensions according to Walter Small's book, *Early New England Schools*, were listed as 20 by 25 feet. Interiors of most schools were usually colorless, and the fact that heating was an everpresent problem was revealed in the prevalent practice of requiring students to provide firewood as part of their tuition. Inadequate maintenance of these undersized buildings was not uncommon, according to this description of one school in 1681: "the glass broke, the floor very much broken and torn up to kindle fires, the hearth spoiled, the seats some burned and others out of kilter, that had well nigh as good keep school in a hog stie as in it."

The achievements of individual schoolmasters varied under such conditions, but at least two seventeenth-century schoolmasters achieved distinction. Elijah Corlett, who held a bachelor's degree from Oxford and a master's from Cambridge, was schoolmaster of the Cambridge, Massachusetts grammar school for 45 years. Students came from all parts of New England to attend his school, and during the final decades of the century this institution reportedly sent more boys to Harvard than did any other school. Ezekiel Cheever had an even lengthier teaching career, "holding the rod for seventy years." Cheever began his teaching career in New Haven in 1638 where he had migrated before taking his degree at Cambridge. Later he taught at Charlestown, Ipswich, and for 38 years at Boston's Latin School before his death in 1708 at age 92. Cheever, who supposedly never missed a school day, was renowned not only for his excellent teaching abilities, but also for his brief but widely used Latin "Accidence." The remarkable educational achievements of both men were extolled in this couplet by Cotton Mather:

Tis Corlett's pains, and *Cheevers* we must own,
That thou, *New England*, art not Scythia grown.

Textbooks

The tools of learning varied in early New England's elementary and secondary schools. The first widely used instructional aid on the elementary level was the so-called "hornbook." The hornbook consisted of a sheet of printed paper about three by four inches, covered with a thin layer of translucent horn. These were then fastened firmly onto a thin, paddle-shaped piece of wood thereby hoping to prolong the usability of this text. On the hornbook paper was usually printed the alphabet in capitals and small letters, the vowels, vowel-consonant combinations, the Lord's Prayer, and the Benediction. A "Battle-door," or enlarged and advanced hornbook, appeared later in the colonial period.

During the closing years of the seventeenth century, the hornbook began to be displaced by the *New England Primer*. Primers had originally appeared before the Reformation as a personal prayer book. By the time of the Great Migration a variety of primers that combined the teaching of reading with the basic tenets of a particular religious sect were prevalent in England. The Puritans brought primers with them, but their diverse religious precepts became a matter of concern to orthodox leaders. The problem was met sometime between 1687 and 1690 by Benjamin Harris, a Boston printer and bookseller, who published the first edition of the *New England Primer*.

Editions of the *New England Primer* differed to some extent in content. Generally, the initial primers contained an approved orthodox catechism such as the Westminster Assembly's "Shorter Catechism." They also contained pages of upper and lower case alphabets, and syllable combinations (viz. ab, eb, ib, ob, ub), used to teach pronunciation. Most early *New England Primers* also contained a list of numbers from 1 to 100, using both Arabic and Roman numerals. In addition, they listed the various books of both Testaments, the Lord's Prayer, the Creed, the Ten Commandments, moral precepts, and an excerpt from John Fox's *Book of Martyrs*. In the most noted section of this *Primer*, the alphabet was taught by the customary method of short, rhymed couplets involving religious or moral precepts. The following examples of this practice from one early *New England Primer* illustrates how this work truly came to be known as "a mirror of Puritanism."

A. In *Adam's* Fall
We sinned All.

B. Thy Life to Mend
This *Book* Attend.

C. The *Cat* doth play
And after slay.

D. A *Dog* will bite
A Thief at night.

E. An *Eagles* flight
Is out of sight.

F. The Idle *Fool*
Is whipt at School.

G. As runs the *Glass*
Mans life doth pass.

H. My *Book* and *Heart*
Shall never part.

J. *Job* feels the Rod
Yet blesses God.

K. Our *King* the good
No man of blood.

L. The *Lion* bold
The *Lamb* doth hold.

M. The *Moon* gives light
In time of night.

N. *Nightingales* sing
In time of Spring

O. The *Royal Oak*
it was the Tree
That sav'd His
Royal Majestie.

P. *Peter* denies
His Lord and Cries.

Q. *Queen Esther* comes
in Royal State
To Save the Jews
from dismal fate.

R. *Rachel* doth mourn
for her first born.

S. *Samuel* annoints
Whom God appoints.

T. *Time* cuts down all
Both great and small.

U. *Uriah's* beauteous wife
Made *David* seek his life.

W. *Whales* in the Sea
God's voice obey.

X. *Xerxes* the great did die,
And so must you & I.

Y. *Youth* forward slips
Death soonest nips.

Z. *Zacheus* he
Did climb the Tree
His Lord to see.

Other texts reflecting this moral and religious tone were employed during this period in several of the elementary level New England schools. The Bible was foremost among the texts. Closely related to the Scriptures were the Psalters, or Books of Psalms, and individual catechisms. One such catechism, *Spiritual Milk for Babes, Drawn out of the Breasts of Both Testaments* was prepared by John Cotton and was widely used throughout Puritan New England. A less widely used work was Michael Wigglesworth's epic poem, *The Day of Doom*, relating the terrors of Judgment Day. While all these works were used at various times and places for elementary instruction, it must be remembered that their distribution in New England was often restricted by the high cost of printing.

The textbooks used in grammar schools were also diverse, but their availability was often restricted by the same factors. In addition to Ezekiel Cheever's "Accidence," a *Nomenclator*, or Latin- English phrasebook, and a vocabulary, or *Sententiae Pueriles*, were used to introduce the boys to the Roman tongue. Later, other works that were read in Latin included Aesop's *Fables*, Erasmus' *Colloquies*, Cicero's *Orations*, and Vergil's *Aeneid*. In schools where Greek was offered in the final year, the most prominent writers studied were Homer, Socrates, and Hesiod. The Bible was also read in both Latin and Greek versions. While most grammar schools lacked this diversity of texts, the schoolmaster did strive with the available material to prepare his students adequately for higher learning.

Higher Education

In October 1636 the Massachusetts General Court appropriated £400 for the establishment of a college. The result of this sudden action, only six years after the start of the Great Migration, marked the beginning of Harvard College. Yet the action of the General Court was not altogether unusual considering the strong Puritan emphasis on learning as well as the concern for the preservation of their orthodox religious and social beliefs. These factors, as well as details regarding the naming of the college are revealed in this excerpt from *New England's First Fruits,* published in 1643.

After God had carried us safe to New England, *and wee had builded our houses, provided necessaries for our liveli-hood, rear'd convenient places for Gods worship, and settled the Civill Government: One of the next things we longed for, and looked after was to advance* Learning *and perpetuate it to Posterity; dreading to leave an illiterate Ministery to the Churches, when our present Ministers shall lie in the Dust. And as wee were thinking and consulting how to effect this great Work, it pleased God to stir up the heart of one Mr.* Harvard *(a godly Gentleman, and a lover of Learning, there living amongst us) to give the one halfe of his Estate (it being in all about 1700.l) towards the erecting of a Colledge: and all his Library: after him another gave 300.l. others after them cast in more, and the publique hand of the State added the rest: the Colledge was, by common consent, appointed to be at Cam-*bridge, *(a place very pleasant and accommodate) and is called (according to the name of the first founder)* Harvard Colledge.

Harvard College led a tempestuous existence for a number of years after its founding. Because of a religious controversy involving Anne Hutchinson, classes did not commence until 1638. The college's first president, Nathanael Eaton, was dismissed for his overly stern discipline and for feeding the students a substandard diet that reportedly included "ungutted mackerel" and "hasty pudding with goats dung in it." Eaton's successor, Henry Dunster, brought stability and higher scholastic standards to Harvard, but he was forced to resign in a controversy over his religious beliefs. Dunster's intellectual vigor was not matched by any other president until the last years of the century when Increase Mather assumed the office.

It was also not until the last two decades of the century that the college obtained enough income from benefactions to keep a permanent teaching force. Most of the college's support came from personal grants, although after 1654 the General Court did assume payment of the president's annual salary. Even so it is not difficult to understand how such perplexing problems kept the number of students who had enrolled at Harvard by 1700 to less than 600 and the average annual graduating class to 8. Even the majority of those who did attend the college lived within a relatively short distance of Cambridge.

By the Massachusetts General Court Charter granted to Harvard in 1650, control over the college deviated somewhat from the model of the residential colleges at Oxford and Cambridge. The ruling powers at Harvard were delegated to two groups, the Corporation and the Overseers. The former group consisted of the president, treasurer, and five fellows called the President and Fellows of Harvard College. This self-perpetuating Corporation was given the academic governing powers of managing the college property, acting for it in law, hiring college servants, and making rules and bylaws for the students. The Overseers consisted of the ministers of Cambridge and the five surrounding towns. While the Corporation was supposed to take the initiative on all important matters, they were expected to obtain the consent of the Overseers who held a veto power. Also, the Corporation was to yield to the Overseers arbitration in cases of substantial disagreement. Although it still held overall academic powers under its charter, the Harvard Corporation proved unable to exercise these rights during the latter half of the seventeenth century. In fact, Morison has written that until the Corporation was reorganized in 1707, "the President governed the College with the aid of such Overseers as were interested, and treated the tutors as senior students assisting him in discipline and instruction rather than as his fellows."

Boys usually entered Harvard from ages 14 to 16. Tuition itself was not disproportionately high, but the general costs and distance from the school did not affect the enrollment. Also, the class rank of enrolling freshmen was usually related to their parents' position in the Puritan social order. Most boys entering Harvard were grammar school graduates, but less than half the graduates of these institutions went on to college in seventeenth-century New England. Those who were not prepared in the grammar schools were privately tutored, usually by the local minister. Entrance requirements were similar to those of English universities. According to Harvard's first college rules adopted in 1642, a student was admitted after he was "able to understand Tully (Cicero), or such like classical author extempore, and make and speake true Latine in verse and prose, *Suo ut aiunt Marte* (by his own effort) and decline perfectly the paradigms of nounes and verbs in the Greek tongue."

The Harvard curriculum was also based on the classically oriented patterns of English universities. The undergraduate courses revolved around the traditional Trivium and Quadrivium but without musical studies, the Three Philosophies (Metaphysics, Ethics, and Natural Science), and Greek, Hebrew, and a chronological study of ancient history. As in English universities logic and rhetoric were the basic subjects in the curriculum. Aristotle and Cicero were the primary classical authors examined, although students became familiar with a wide variety of writers from the ancient to the contemporary. Composition, orations, and disputations were given the same careful scrutiny as at English universities while senior theses invariably carried a religious topic. After graduation students could stay on for further theological studies and a master's degree.

Undergraduates were ruled by a strict disciplinary code. Stringent control over their conduct continued after the dismissal of President Eaton. Henry Dunster's rigid code of 1642 was, in fact, largely an imitation of the exacting rules he had known as a Cambridge undergraduate. Students were ranked according to scholastic merit, but all were obliged to follow the circumscribed college laws. Among other requirements students were compelled to show punctilious attendance for classes and religious worship; they were restricted in travel outside the university; and they were required to give absolute, unquestioned obedience to faculty members. Fines and whippings were the most common punishment for rule violations, but some students did suffer expulsion during this period.

One of the principal motives behind the founding of Harvard had been a concern for ministerial training, but this did not mean that its graduates invariably became pastors. Broader educational goals than those of a mere theological seminary were stated in the charter of 1650, which admonished the college to seek the advancement of "all good literature arts and Sciences." According to a study by Richard Hofstader, only about 52 percent of Harvard's seventeenth-century graduates entered the ministry. The remainder followed a multiplicity of occupations including farming, law, medicine, teaching, and commerce. Indeed, Harvard College had come to serve as a training ground for the leaders of Puritan society in a manner that far outweighed the small number of scholars it enrolled.

Girls' Education

Although women were rated below men in the social hierarchy, Puritan beliefs concerning saving faith made no distinction with respect to sex. Women, as well as men, were predestined to eternal salvation or to eternal damnation, so that both sexes were expected to be given a knowledge and understanding of the Scriptures and to pass them on to their children. In addition, Puritans anticipated that both boys and girls would be bound out as apprentices to learn a calling. Educational statutes reflected their basic concern for complete economic, religious, and social security. The educational obligations on parents and masters in Massachusetts' Law of 1642 made no distinction according to sex, and the Old Deluder Law of 1647 stated specifically that on the elementary level, teachers were to instruct "all such children as shall resort to him to read and write." Similar laws in other Puritan colonies also made it incumbent that girls be acquainted with elementary learning.

Boys and girls attended the dame schools and town schools

of early New England. In dame schools, girls were sometimes taught sewing and cooking in addition to learning the letters and reading with the boys. Town schools, taught by men, did not offer such domestic training. In fact, discrimination between the sexes sometimes was made by these elementary institutions. Dorchester, Massachusetts in 1639 instituted a special committee to determine "whether maids shall be taught with boys or not," while Deerfield later excluded girls over 10 from its town schools. Lynn and Medford, Massachusetts allowed girls to attend their town schools only after the boys' afternoon dismissal, and some towns admitted girls in the summer but not winter months. While such distinctions did appear in several town schools, there appear to have been few attempts to deny girls any equal acquaintanceship with reading and writing at this elementary level.

Secondary education was another matter. Most Puritans believed that women lacked the strength for more-advanced intellectual exercises and girls were not formally prepared for college regardless of the mental abilities they might have displayed during their elementary education. Consequently, New England's public Latin grammar schools were closed to girls. New Haven's Hopkins Grammar School made a formal statement to this effect in 1680, but generally no such edicts were needed to exclude girls from these secondary schools.

This did not mean that no girl in seventeenth century New England received any secondary instruction. A few Puritan ministers, such as John Williams of Deerfield, tutored their daughters as well as their sons in Latin and Greek. Also, there were private schools in a few towns such as Boston and Newport where, for a fee, girls might be instructed in secondary level subjects. According to Clifford Shipton, one of the most prominent private secondary schools in Boston was conducted by Peter Burr from 1695 to 1699. Cotton Mather sent his daughter to Burr's school to learn Latin, and girls as well as boys came from distant towns to study at this school. By the close of the seventeenth century, however, the relative number of such schools was still small, and only a few privileged girls had gone beyond the limits of elementary learning and domestic training.

Girls' education was only one part of this remarkable educational system established in seventeenth-century New England. Like England, from which it inherited much of its formal and informal learning patterns, New England's educational system reflected the society and the social order within which it existed. Yet in Puritan New England advances were made beyond English educational theory and practice. Through their intense religious beliefs Puritans had given a special emphasis to orthodox learning within their sectarian dominated communities. This emphasis on education was augmented in their New World settlements by fears of an imminent collapse of their family structure within their hostile new environment. As a result, the Puritan colonies recognized a state responsibility for education that was unknown in England. Mandatory education laws, such as those passed by the Massachusetts legislature, had set the basis for a town-controlled system of compulsory education and compulsory schools for children of its communities.

Universal compliance with Puritan educational statutes was not achieved but, by the close of the seventeenth century, a substantial number of town-supported elementary and secondary schools, along with a well established college, were operating. These educational achievements and a literacy rate surpassing England's were attained in spite of the restrictive conditions of a frontier society, serious Indian warfare, and divisive internal and external controversies. Puritan determination by 1700 had indeed engendered a notable educational structure.

new england education in the eighteenth century (1700-1776)

The New England colonies experienced significant economic, social, religious, and intellectual changes during the years of the eighteenth century that preceded the American Revolution. While governmental structures remained relatively static throughout this period, important changes occurred in other areas that were drastically transforming the New England environment. A rapid population growth was one observable factor affecting these changes: from an estimated 130,000 inhabitants in 1700, the population of the region increased to almost 600,000 without large-scale immigration from Europe. As a result of this population growth urban life increased in towns such as Boston and Newport. At the same time, smaller communities experienced a dispersal of settlement away from the original pattern around the town common to all parts of the entire township. Such demographic factors, however, reflect only one of several influences on the overall alterations in the economic, social, religious, and intellectual life of eighteenth-century New Englanders. By the eve of the American Revolution, the widespread changes in these fields in effect transformed the cooperative and well-ordered Puritans of the seventeenth century into independent, revitalized, and individualistic "Yankees."

It was inevitable that the earlier educational practices of the region would be affected by such pervasive changes. The advanced educational system that was established in seventeenth-century New England—outside of Rhode Island—had been expected to complement and sustain Puritan religious and social concepts. Compulsory education statutes, compulsory school maintenance laws, and the operation of the schools themselves all reflected the existing Puritan order. When this order underwent extensive alterations, its educational structure was obliged to change its form to meet the needs of these new situations.

Economic and Social Change

Beginning in the final years of the seventeenth century, New England's economic interests started to outgrow its localized base of farming and fishing. This rapid growth of new economic opportunities—which had its fullest development in the eighteenth century—found New England commercial ventures spreading over vast reaches of the Atlantic Ocean. Under the direction of wealthy merchant capitalists, Yankee ships carried livestock, fish, wheat, lumber, rum, and other products to the West Indies, Europe, and the African coast. The original bilateral trade for finished English products now broadened to include traffic in molasses, sugar, ivory, gold dust, and African slaves. Commerce became fixed as the great source of New England's growing prosperity and the trading activities of its bustling coastal communities were barometers of the economic well-being of the region. Thus, even before the American Revolution, towns as Boston, Portsmouth, Newport, and New Haven had come to represent the flourishing and wealthy centers of commercial and urban life.

The increased wealth accumulated in New England's urban centers was often invested in local commercial enterprises or was utilized for land speculation. In the former instance, rum manufacturing offered a very profitable item for the export trade; by 1750, 15,000 gallons were reportedly exported from Massachusetts alone. Shipbuilding and lumber industries were other fields of investment for new capital and skilled labor. Simultaneously, the abandonment of traditional communal landowning practices for individual proprietorship paved the way for a widespread outburst of land speculation throughout much of New England. Affluent individuals, or groups of investors, purchased extensive tracts of land or obtained sizable land grants from the colonial assembly and sold them to settlers at a profit. Conflicts often occurred between the nonresident proprietors and settlers, but the speculation in land did serve as a means of absorbing surplus capital and diffusing property among the increased population.

As the region's principal occupations, farming and fishing were significantly affected by the rapid economic changes. In a recent study, Richard Bushman has shown that a growing number of New England farmers were entering trade and becoming "marginal producers" during the eighteenth century. Many of these farmers conducted side businesses within their communities or peddled their products to established merchants in larger urban communities. At times the newer farmer-traders quarreled with the older merchants over financial or other issues, yet in the long run both groups served to promote economic development. Fishing also aided commercial growth. Besides providing a source of employment for seamen, the ever-growing amount of fish catches gave urban merchants a readily exportable product for a profitable market in Europe and the West Indies. During the eighteenth century many established merchants capitalized on such opportunities, thereby creating the foundations for a number of personal fortunes.

The emergence of this new mercantile gentry helped alter New England's social structure. Families such as the Fanieuls, Olivers, Hutchinsons, and Quincys, who had acquired considerable fortunes through commerce or speculation, joined magistrates, physicians, and lawyers at the apex of the class pyramid. As this combined grouping came to dominate the social ladder, many ministers slipped to a more "middling" level. Here, certain pastors now found themselves ranked with the newer tradesmen-farmers, artisans, and others of a middle-class status. The lowest societal level, often designated the "inferior sort," consisted of poorer farmers, indentured servants, unskilled urban laborers, and at the very bottom, Negro slaves and Indians. Within all of these class levels, social stratifications increased during the eighteenth century.

Paralleling these changes in social class structure was an intensifying concern over class status. In a sermon in 1738, *The Fall of the Mighty Lamented*, the Reverend Samuel Mather reflected a commonly held attitude toward social inequality: "It appears very evident that the Supreme Governor of the World has been pleas'd to constitute a Difference in Families: For while most of the Sons of Men are Brethren of low Degree or of common Derivation: Some are Sons and Daughters of the Mighty." Those who considered themselves within this temporal category of the "Mighty" often sought to display evidence of their position. Throughout the later colonial period emblems of upper class preeminence appeared in many facets: stately homes, beautiful clothes, domestic servants and, most significantly, a private education for children.

Such meaningful social changes however, did not result in social harmony. As the new merchant-dominated upper class strove to press its claims to economic, political, and social superiority, its members were often challenged by those of the middle and lower orders. These latter social groups refused to accept the Old World concept of abject subordination to one's betters and they insisted that the roadways of opportunity and social mobility remain open. Resultant class conflicts emerged over various issues: agitation by farmers and debtors for issues of cheap paper currency; contentions over land ownership and land grants; and struggles for control of town and colony elective officers. These and other instances of class antagonism continued and even grew as the American Revolution approached. In all, they reflected the growth of an independent, practical, and democratic Yankee spirit.

The manifestations of such social and economic changes were not entirely uniform throughout New England. Generally, the transitions were more apparent in larger coastal communities than in frontier settlements. Social class differences often were not as sharply defined in rural as in more urban areas, while in some cases, sectional or political factors intervened to ameliorate class or economic rivalries. Nonetheless, the impact of new social and economic forces had brought change and, combined with other factors, they had considerably transformed the fundamental institutions of the region.

Religious and Intellectual Change

Religious life in New England was particularly affected by the growing economic and social transition. The rapid commercial development, the rise in accumulated wealth, and the emergence of a mercantile gentry all contributed to a rising secular outlook that modified the earlier predominance of religious thought. Evidence of this increasing secularization and decreasing piety were especially noted by the clergy. In 1707 the Reverend Cotton Mather warned of the dangers of excessive temporal amibition: "When Wealth is more unto us than the Creator of all our Wealth; Here, Here is the Criminal Covetousness." Other ministers were equally concerned about the increased profaneness of secular concerns, citing such scriptural admonitions as, "What shall it profit a man if he gain the whole world and lose his own soul." Yet more and more New Englanders during this period were ignoring these divine precepts in their pursuit of social or economic gain. The failure to halt this secular trend, particularly evident in larger towns, invariably meant a continued decay of older orthodox patterns.

Other factors also influenced the declining importance of religion during the early eighteenth century. Many Congregational churches were seriously weakened by rifts over doctrine, polity, and other issues. Simultaneously, attempts to avoid such quarrels through compromise solutions failed to produce religious harmony. Ecclesiastical bickering continued within congregations and church membership was awarded more and more on a voluntary basis rather than on proven piousness. At the same time, more college graduates were avoiding the ministry as a profession, so that the pulpits were often left to men unable to follow the leadership capacities shown by the first generation of Puritan pastors. Ministers and laymen alike were guilty of moral laxity, impiety, and a disrespect for law and authority. In short, by the 1730s much of New England's religious life had been subverted by this mood of spiritual deadness.

A reaction to this mood of spiritual decay was evinced during the Great Awakening of the 1730s and 1740s. This celebrated religious revival swept through the American colonies but was particularly strong in New England. There evangelical leaders such as Jonathan Edwards and George Whitefield rekindled long-absent flames of religious enthusiasm and personal piety. Thousands attended meetings where revivalists instilled the fear of impending divine punishment on those guilty of excessive worldliness. Many inhabitants renounced their temporal holdings and sought a renewed experience of conversion. Few New England towns escaped these and other pervasive effects of the Great Awakening.

The overall effects of the revival were far more enduring than the temporary religious hysteria that often gripped communities. Quite significantly, the Great Awakening had formally split the Congregational churches between an antirevivalist Old Light faction and a prorevivalist New Light faction. Their differences often led dissident factions into establishing their own congregations that weakened the standing religious order of both Connecticut and Massachusetts. The weakening of these sectarian establishments was matched by a rise in religious toleration, the spread of a new missionary zeal, and a renewed emergence of humanitarianism and individualism. The revival also assisted the growth of the region's minority Protestant sects, such as Baptists, Quakers, and Episcopalians. Preoccupation with secular concerns was checked only temporarily by the Awakening, but the basic institutions of New England, including education, experienced its effects long after the religious fervor subsided.

Intellectual developments in New England were related to the Great Awakening. The European Enlightenment, which began toward the end of the seventeenth century, soon spread its influence to the American colonies, primarily through books, pamphlets, almanacs, and other printed matter. Most New England pastors had welcomed the movement believing that its Newtonian precepts might reinforce religious orthodoxy. Ironically, however, the Enlightenment's accentuation of man's independent rationality and its repudiation of supernatural explanations of phenomena invariably weakened rather than strengthened spiritual conformity. In this way the new learning served as a catalyst for the Great Awakening. During the revival its intellectual doctrines of individualism and natural liberty were repeatedly used by Jonathan Edwards and other leading evangelists.

Aside from its religious effects, the Enlightenment brought a fresh intellectual outlook to American colonists. In New England this was particularly evident in the growing urban centers and among the middle and upper classes. There the new learning, although modified and refined by the American environment, had broadened the circumscribed perspectives restricting the thought of the early settlers. The works of Newton, Locke, Montesquieu, Gibbon, and other European notables confronted New England readers with surprising new concepts and unfamiliar situations. For many of the colonists, the result meant replacing their traditional doctrinal attitudes with a more inquisitive and worldly vitality.

Manifestations of New England's expanding artistic and intellectual temper were exemplified in other ways. Painters such as John Smibert, Robert Feke, and John Singleton Copley sparked a broadening interest in art; architectural styles were brought into new grace through the skill of Peter Harrison; in music the secular compositions of European masters were being performed in concert or recital. Sciences as well as the fine arts also progressed during this period. John Winthrop IV made significant investigations and observations in mathematics and astronomy; the Reverend Jared Eliot wrote several tracts on agronomy; in medicine, Doctor Zabdiel Boylston experimented with smallpox inoculations.

These studies, along with other writings from the American and European Enlightenment gained broad dissemination through an increasing number of private printers in the region. All of the larger communities usually had at least one print shop where books, pamphlets, almanacs, and informative newspapers were published and distributed. Sometimes urban centers also proffered the new knowledge by means of large individual collections or through public libraries such as Newport's impressive Redwood Library. Through these and other means, therefore, the more educated and urbanized New Englanders were slowly but steadily assimilating the styles and precepts of a new era in modern thought.

Education and Change in New England

It was previously noted that the structure of education in seventeenth-century New England was directly related to the backgrounds, needs, and desires of its early inhabitants. Fearing the possible destruction of cherished religious and social beliefs, the Puritan colonies had transplanted modified versions of the classically oriented educational institutions of England. The resultant educational order was counted on to maintain and perpetuate Puritan ideals, while the legislatures instituted colonywide standards that they expected local officials to enforce. Even Rhode Island, whose assembly disregarded education completely during the seventeenth century, possessed a few schools based on Old World models.

In the eighteenth century, however, the rapid and pervasive changes which altered the environment of most New Englanders necessitated new additions to traditional learning practices. The earlier uniform and placid educational order, designed to promote Puritan religious and social interests, could not remain amidst the pressures of a more volatile, mobile, and secularly oriented society. Inhabitants still preserved their basic faith in learning but now sought to broaden the ends of education within these new societal attitudes. As the spirit of religion declined and the influences of commercialization and intellectualism gained, many communities sought novel educational concepts or institutions to meet their new situations. For example, the rising necessity for broader vocational training and the growing accentuation of utilitarianism weakened the predominance of classically oriented curricula. The Old World ideal of the aristocratic gentleman and classical scholar still remained, but for middle-class artisans, merchants, and the farmer-tradesmen practical studies were far more essential to their needs. In elementary schooling, therefore, modifications were often made in order to satisfy the changing requirements of the settlers. At the secondary level, however, the public Latin grammar school proved unable to evolve from its circumscribed classical base so that the expansion of private secondary instruction became a most significant educational development of the eighteenth century.

The steady broadening of private education, as well as other aspects of education, varied in extent throughout the region. While most communities responded with little difficulty to the emergent demands for greater vocational training, a few towns endeavored to preserve the older forms of learning. In addition, although some communities retained their original, publicly supported school system, other towns abandoned or weakened their obligations. During this period, colleges also instituted innovations while retaining many of their original features.

Compulsory Education

In the previous chapter it was noted that during the seventeenth century all the New England colonies but Rhode Island
had moved to establish a system of compulsory education.
Commencing with the Massachusetts Bay General Court in
1642, statutes were enacted obligating both parents and masters
to provide their children or apprentices with at least a basic
instruction in reading. These mandatory education acts had
reflected the intense Puritan concern for learning. By the outbreak of King Philip's War in 1675, legislatures in all Puritan
colonies had enacted similar legislation and left enforcement
to the individual towns.

In Massachusetts the abandonment of this system of compulsory education started even before the beginning of the
eighteenth century. During the brief, authoritarian rule of the
Dominion of New England (1685–1689), a statute was enacted
that, in effect, revoked all existing mandatory education
statutes. After the Dominion of New England was overturned
and Plymouth Colony was absorbed into Massachusetts under
a royal charter, the new Bay Colony legislature in 1692 tried
to reconfirm all colonial laws existing prior to 1685. One
statute enacted for this purpose would have included the
restoration of all former compulsory education acts, but this
statute was disallowed when it was sent to England for review.
Throughout the remainder of the colonial period the Massachusetts legislature made no further attempt to enforce mandatory education for all children, including the apprenticing of
illiterate children. A law that was enacted in 1692 allowed
selectmen to apprentice indigent children to masters who were
obligated to teach them to read and write, but its provisions
were weakened by subsequent legislation in 1710.

Somewhat similar trends occurred in the other Puritan
colonies. The Connecticut Colony government, which regained
its corporate status after the overthrow of the Dominion of
New England, enacted a bill in 1690 designed to restore most of

its original compulsory educational policies. Recognizing wide-spread reading deficiencies, the act of 1690 made it incumbent upon local jurymen to examine the reading ability of all the town's children, and it provided fines for negligent parents or masters. Twelve years later a revised colony legal code tempered these requirements by allowing negligent parents or masters to escape a fine by teaching their children "a short catechism." Later, simply the memorization of such a catechism could be substituted for a reading ability so that by the end of the colonial period, Connecticut, like Massachusetts, had no mandatory education statutes in force.

New Hampshire followed a similar course, with similar legislation. For several years after its separation from Massachusetts in 1691, New Hampshire lacked any compulsory education laws, but in 1712 an act allowed town selectmen to check the reading ability of all children above age 10. Those youths who were unable to read could be apprenticed, but significantly, town officials were not compelled to take such action. A later statute in 1766 paralleled the Massachusetts Laws of 1692 and 1710 by permitting the apprenticing of poor children and requiring that only male apprentices be instructed in both reading and writing. Despite the provisions of these laws, enforcement was weak and one eighteenth-century New Hampshire writer admitted that for poor children, "methods were found to evade the law."

Rhode Island's government, which never was an instrument of religious policy, remained true to its earlier position regarding compulsory education. Prior to the American Revolution, its legislature took no action to require any form of mandatory education within the colony.

Except for Rhode Island, which adhered to its initial policy of educational indifference, the trend toward the abandonment of compulsory education requirements was quite apparent. There were many factors causing colonial legislatures to slacken their efforts in this direction. The decline in the earlier religious zeal, the absence of the former church-state harmony in Puritan colonies, and the rapid commercialization of society all contributed to the same result. While citizens still preserved their basic faith in educational standards, and while public schools actually improved during the eighteenth century, none of the New England colonies retained the legal statutes that had enforced their previous mandatory educational policies.

Compulsory School Maintenance Legislation

The fate of compulsory school maintenance statutes in eighteenth-century New England colonies differed somewhat from that of compulsory education legislation. It will be recalled that Massachusetts' "Old Deluder" Law of 1647 had literally legislated schools into existence by requiring towns of 50 families or more to offer instruction in reading and writing, and towns of over 100 families to establish a Latin grammar school. This act, which provided mandatory fines on delinquent communities, had become a model for all New England colonies but Rhode Island. During the last decades of the seventeenth century, however, a growing number of towns—particularly those on the isolated frontier—were not complying with these mandatory school maintenance statutes. These negligent communities were not indifferent to education, but the desolation caused by Indian warfare and the scarcity of teachers often hindered its fulfillment. The Massachusetts General Court appeared particularly unsympathetic to this growing situation, and in 1692 it strongly reasserted the requirements of the 1647 statute and doubled the fine for noncompliance to £10 for larger towns.

In Massachusetts the tendency toward a strict legislative reaffirmation of the town's responsibility for schooling continued into the eighteenth century despite rising evasions. The General Court in 1701 increased the fine from £10 to £20 on those towns failing to maintain a required grammar school. In 1718 the penalties were further increased; towns of 150 families or more were to pay £30 for noncompliance, towns of 200 families were to pay £40, and towns of 300 families £60. As Robert Middlekauff has noted, such statutes were designed "to make the penalty higher than a master's salary" since "many towns preferred paying a fine to supporting a master." Many communities, however, were still unable to conform to these stiffening colonywide standards. During Queen Anne's War (1702–1713) frontier towns such as Billerica and Marlborough pleaded to the courts that the dangers of Indian raids prevented their compliance with school statutes, while other towns such as Andover and Malden claimed a lack of funds to pay a teacher. As the century progressed, many other Massachusetts communities found reason to request exemptions from these laws, and several towns deliberately closed their schools for varying periods of time.

The objectives of compulsory school legislation in eighteenth century Connecticut and New Hampshire was similar to, though the specific terms of their statutes often differed from, those of Massachusetts. In 1690 the Connecticut General Court had required only Hartford and New Haven to maintain grammar schools and obligated towns of over thirty families to keep a reading and writing school for only six months annually. A stricter law in 1700 restored the earlier requirement for grammar schools in each of the four county towns and now required towns with more than 70 families to keep year-round reading and writing schools. Smaller communities were expected to maintain such schools at least six months annually. Delinquent towns would not be fined but would lose the benefits from a share in colonywide taxation. In 1717 the Connecticut legislature transferred the elementary level requirements of this act from the entire town to the individual parish, and these revisions continued throughout the remainder of the colonial period.

In 1693 the New Hampshire legislature had required all but one of its towns to maintain a reading and writing school under penalty of a £10 fine. Since this statute made no mention of the lack of Latin grammar schools, and since public pressures for one increased, the General Court acted in 1708 to establish such an institution. Legislation that year established the school in Portsmouth, but the stipulation that it was to be supported by all the leading towns proved unpopular. In the meantime, the growing failure of towns to maintain any schools caused the General Court to return to a strict policy. In 1719 the legislature passed a bill quite similar to the "Old Deluder" statute, but with a stiffer £20 penalty. Two years later, another statute made grammar schools mandatory in all parishes with over 100 families, with the selectmen personally liable for penalities of up to £20 for noncompliance. These two acts remained in force throughout the American Revolution, but their observance was far from complete.

It can be surmised from these facts that enacting compulsory school legislation and enforcing such statutes were two distinct problems during the eighteenth century. As previously mentioned, the scarcity of qualified masters, a lack of funds, and the dangers of living on the exposed frontier were among the pleas used by towns for their default in maintaining schools. But there were additional factors limiting the degree of enforcement. The older, closeknit patterns of settlement collapsed as inhabitants moved away from the town center and established new parishes within the township. This dispersal of population, combined with the overall decline of religious zeal and the increased predominance of secular concerns, further weakened the state's determinative role in educational practices. Although most inhabitants preserved their basic faith in learning, many towns preferred to pay fines rather than to hire more-costly masters, and an even greater number of towns sought to evade both establishing schools and paying fines. In particular, towns were more neglectful about establishing the less-utilitarian grammar schools than the reading and writing schools. The courts in New England usually were more aware of these limitations than were the legislators and consequently tempered their judicial power with discretion.

The declining local enforcement of compulsory legislation,

particularly for grammar schools, was quite evident in Massachusetts. In 1708, for example, only four of nine towns in Middlesex County with over 100 families were maintaining a grammar school. Worcester County communities showed even greater laxity; during a 34-year period 18 towns were cited for failure to support grammar schools. Also, because some justices were lenient, many of those towns that were actually brought before local courts were able to avoid paying a fine. Thus, Westford, Haverhill, and Groton on occasion convinced the justices that they lacked the requisite 100 families for a grammar school. Lancaster successfully used the excuse that their schoolmaster was temporarily ill while Portland cited their inability to find a master. Although the Hampshire County courts in western Massachusetts proved generally more strict about compliance, several towns in other counties disregarded the statutes for brief periods without any response from local justices.

The effects of this indifference or resistance toward compulsory grammar school requirements were apparent by the final years of the colonial period. Even though the Massachusetts General Court had often complained about the number of towns neglecting to establish grammar schools and had stiffened existing mandatory legislation, the enforcement procedures were not uniformly applied by local officials. In 1765 only 48 out of 140 towns of 100 or more families in Massachusetts were said to maintain grammar schools. Given the reasonable accuracy of this estimate, it is obvious that obedience to the law and support for grammar schools had fallen into serious decline by the eve of the American Revolution.

Connecticut and New Hampshire, with their own school maintenance laws, also met enforcement difficulties during the eighteenth century. In Connecticut legal compliance was greater than in Massachusetts, but it must be remembered that Connecticut's compulsory school laws were less stringent than those of the Bay Colony. Of the four county grammar schools required by the statute of 1700, only Fairfield proved unable to maintain its school. The Fairfield school closed in 1752 after a proposal for raising needed financial assistance was rejected by the General Assembly. Generally, the other county towns were able to maintain their grammar schools although Hartford and New London encountered substantial problems. Relatively few Connecticut parishes were cited for failing to offer elementary instruction.

While New Hampshire's school laws were more strict than Connecticut's, their enforcement also lagged. The statute of 1708, which had established a grammar school in Portsmouth supported by the colony towns, was abandoned nine years later. The school was reopened by community effort only after the town had been cited for failure to maintaine a schoolmaster. The act of 1721, requiring grammar schools in parishes with over 100 families, was, as Middlekauff states, "never an unqualified success." Some towns refused to support schools; courts generally failed to enforce the law; and even the General Court became more indifferent. In 1771 acknowledgement of such educational apathy was obvious when the legislature cut the penalties in half for parishes not maintaining schools.

Throughout the entire colonial period Rhode Island enacted no statutes requiring parishes or towns to maintain schools. Yet the colony was not completely indifferent to education. An increasing number of communities were voluntarily supporting some form of public schooling and in 1769 a Providence town meeting even voted "to build three schoolhouses for small children and one for youth to provide instruction, and pay the expense from the treasury."

School Financing and School Administration

Seventeenth-century procedures for financing education were carried over into the following century. By the provisions of the Massachusetts School Law of 1647 and similar statutes in other Puritan colonies, legislatures had left to the communities themselves the means of supporting mandatory town schools and schoolmasters. Individual towns had complied in various ways. Most of them had paid their school costs through local taxes supplemented by student fees. Many communities had also used land grants, gifts, and contributions to offset the rather considerable expense of establishing and maintaining schools. Such methods for meeting the costly burden of education persisted during the eighteenth century, although a number of towns now sought new forms of financial support. Nevertheless, the principle that the community itself could choose whatever means it saw fit to support education continued throughout the entire colonial period.

The broadening means of educational financing which occurred during the eighteenth century was linked directly to New England's pervasive economic and social changes. As the earlier closeknit Puritan social order collapsed, and a wider, more secularly oriented social structure emerged, the general community willingness to finance public education receded. Regular support for a system of popular schooling seemed less essential. Also, there was the problem of the availability of money itself within many communities. Although the economy of New England expanded and its wealth increased, the cost of education remained high. Hard currency was scarce and inflationary trends reduced the actual income value of many towns' fixed educational investments. A search for new means of financial assistance therefore resulted.

Many New England towns did find new sources of monetary support for education. Some communities received temporary relief from their increased educational burdens through reinvesting school funds into more profitable ventures. Other towns lightened educational burdens through sizeable bequests or gifts. In Connecticut, the school law of 1700 gave towns that maintained schools annual grants from a tax of "forty shillings upon every thousand pounds of the public list of persons and estates unto the several towns of this colony." Forty-one years later the legislature distributed among all existing parishes the funds received from an earlier sale of seven unsettled townships, and in 1750 it created a permanent school fund. New Hampshire also used land grants in efforts to maintain local schooling. During the eighteenth century concerned communities in New England placed taxes on items such as liquor, taverns, gristmills, and ferries in efforts to obtain sufficient funds for education. As the colonial period concluded, however, the overall sucess of the tax programs was limited and the school financial crisis had become even more critical.

While the problems of educational financing intensified, the forms of school administration in New England were evolving in new directions. The earliest and most common means of local school control during the seventeenth century had been the town meeting. Later, the individual town meetings began to share much of their school authority with the town selectmen, and in 1693 Massachusetts made both groups jointly responsible for education.

As communities grew in size and complexity during the later colonial period, towns tended to rely on special school committees or committees of selectmen to administer the educational policies formulated at the town meeting. Such school committees had been used occasionally during the seventeenth century, but after the first quarter of the eighteenth century, they were used with far more regularity, often becoming standing committees. Their membership usually included the more prominent members of the community—selectment, ministers, and justices—who were appointed, or more often elected, to these positions. The powers of these regular or standing school committees steadily increased over those of individual selectmen, and by the end of the colonial period they were frequently the chief agency for local school supervision.

School committees supervised such educational functions as selection of school sites, hiring a schoolmaster, and school construction and maintenance. The most important duties, however, usually fell to the school inspection committee.

Originally, school inspections were made through informal ministerial calls or by a single selectman who made cursory visits to the local schools. By the early years of the eighteenth century many New England towns began appointing temporary committees to inspect their schools, and in 1714 the Connecticut legislature requested local officials to visit and report on their school at least four times annually. The early, informal school inspection committees usually consisted of selectmen, ministers, and other prominent residents. As the century proceded, however, towns began to delegate the task of visitation to specifically appointed individuals who were expected to report on their findings. In Boston, the school visitation became such a popular social function, and the size of the regular inspection committee grew to large, that it eventually became unwieldy and inefficient. Usually, a local pastor was included as a member of the inspection committee although Boston's committee came to consist only of selectmen and whoever they chose to accompany them.

Paralleling the emergence of school committees was the decentralization of the town school system and the emergence of the district system. The inhabitants of New England's original towns were invariably clustered together in a single compact settlement within the extensive town grant. Sometimes, fears of Indian attacks caused towns to forbid families to live more than a short distance from the meetinghouse. However, as the dangers of Indian attacks receded, and as communities grew in population and self-sufficiency, many inhabitants began moving to the town's outlying sections. Here new settlers not only established their own farms and villages but they also formed their own churches and petitioned to become a distinct parish or district with the rights of local self-government. One right that outlying parishes claimed was control over education since the settlers were usually taxed to support schools, and since colony laws, except for Rhode Island, required schools. Because these newer settlements were often located at some distance from the original town school with the accompanying difficulties of travel, many distant parishes declined to pay school taxes and established their own schools.

The resultant loss of income threatened the finances of the original town school, and residents of the early settlements soon sought compromise with the newer parishes.

The response to the educational demands of these outlying parishes came initially in the form of so-called "moving schools." Under this moving school system the town school-master traveled from parish to parish in the town, offering varying periods of instruction. Support for the moving school came largely from taxes so that the length of instruction usually depended on the amount of school rates paid by a particular settlement. The system became quite prevalent in New England after 1725 and, according to a study by Harlan Updegraff, several Massachusetts towns such as Tisbury, Weston, and Fitchburg adopted moving schools as their first town school. Many other communities switched to the system, as exemplified by this excerpt from the minutes of a Harvard, Massachusetts town meeting in 1740:

Voted, to have the school for the future in the quarters.

Voted, that each quarter shall have a quarter of the money spent in schooling among themselves, as it shall be granted from time to time.

Voted, that each quarter shall find or build a convenient house to keep the school in.

Voted, that the selectmen shall have full power in order the school in each quarter, from time to time; it is to be understood that if one quarter has the school in a good time, then to have it next in time not so good, as it shall be judged by the selectmen, who are fully empowered to manage said affair.

Voted, that if any quarter neglects to build or procure a convenient house to keep the school in, when it comes to their turn, the school shall be kept in the next quarter whose turn it would be.

Moving schools, however, proved inadequate for meeting the

educational needs of an entire town. They were often undependable or irregular in their operation and often gave severely limited instruction. In Yarmouth, Massachusetts the moving school was kept in five places varying from one to four months at each location, while in Sutton, Massachusetts the moving school was kept at four sites. Also, many towns used elementary writing schools as their moving school in outlying sections, while keeping the grammar school within the original town settlement. As a result of such shortcomings, many parishes or districts began to demand and receive their portion of school taxes or funds to spend as they pleased. This district system of control emerged in New England during the latter half of the eighteenth century and was formally legalized by Connecticut in 1766 and by Massachusetts in 1789.

The decentralization of school control to the district level represented a democratic response to the educational needs of a dispersed town population. It allowed each section of a town to determine for itself the nature of schooling that its children received, and it enabled the district to hire its own schoolmaster. In addition, the district school, like the moving school, represented at least nominal conformity to compulsory statutes. However, the dissemination of school administration from town committees to district control was not without its adverse effects on the quality of learning. The smaller and poorer districts were often limited to short school terms and inferior teaching. Yet despite such evident shortcomings, New England's district school system remained a fixed educational institution until long after the American Revolution.

Informal Educational Patterns

The basic features of informal education in New England endured throughout the later colonial period. The family continued to serve as an infant's initial guide to morality and religion, while the apprenticeship system remained the principal means of informal training for a child's vocational calling.

The apprenticeship system was still controlled by statute although many later colonial laws were less stringent in content. During the eighteenth century, for example, apprenticeship legislation in Massachusetts limited those children who could be apprenticed to those of the more indigent families, and it did not provide penalties on town officials for failure to apprentice. These subsequent statutes also departed from the theological aims of earlier apprenticeship laws by failing to require instruction in religion for all children. Throughout most of the eighteenth century Connecticut was in fact the only New England colony to compel religious instruction.

While apprenticeship legislation became generally more permissive, the essential scope of apprenticeship in New England broadened considerably. The extensive economic changes of the eighteenth century, combined with the growing utilitarian outlook, brought an enlarged base for vocational education. Apprenticeship training was extended in law, medicine, trade, and commerce to meet the expanded professional and technical needs of the new society. Most of the apprentices' training was acquired on the job, as in the case of Benjamin Franklin who was apprenticed to a printer at age 12. Robert F. Seybolt in his study of apprenticeship education appointed out, however, that by the eighteenth century "many apprentices were learning at school not only reading and writing, but also part of their trade education." In addition, some masters in larger towns were using evening schools to supplement their apprentices' training. This increased emphasis on vocational education remained in America beyond the colonial period.

Elementary and Secondary Education

The principal aspects of elementary and secondary schooling in eighteenth-century New England were also affected by the widespread societal changes. As previously noted, the earlier patterns of school administration, school financing, and school legislation were altered in the face of new environmental forces. This too was the case within elementary and secondary education itself. While many seventeenth-century instructional features persisted during the later colonial period, there were also significant transitions from earlier elementary and secondary educational patterns.

There were many such admixtures of tradition and transition at the elementary educational level. Dame schools still existed, but they were being gradually absorbed into a single-town school system. While a few large communities such as Boston were able to maintain year-round elementary schools, the general dispersion of population and the adoption of the moving school system often resulted in very brief school terms. The limited elementary curriculum was still dominated by reading and writing, within a sectarian orientation, but instruction in arithmetic, or ciphering, was emerging into greater prominence. For example, Massachusetts in 1741 added ciphering to the mandatory instruction that was offered to male apprentices living outside the bounds of any town and, after 1771, to those entering one town from another. Most New England communities, however, offered basic instruction in arithmetic as a result of popular demand rather than through legal statutes. Their feelings in this respect were a further reflection of local attempts to adjust to the more complex technical needs of their changing society.

Elementary schools themselves were still conducted within an austere environment. When not held in a private home or possibly in a meetinghouse, the local schoolbuilding was usually of poor construction. The following excerpt describes one such rural Connecticut school during the later eighteenth century:

The schoolhouse chimney was of stone, and the fireplace was six feet wide and four deep. The flue was so ample and so perpendicular that the rain, sleet, and snow fell directly to the hearth. In winter the battle for life with green sizzling fuel, which was brought in lengths and cut up by the scholars, was a stern one. Not infrequently the wood, gushing with sap as it was, chanced to let the fire go out, and as there was no living without fire, the school was dismissed, whereat all the scholars rejoiced.

At the secondary level of education, the emergent utilitarian-vocational outlook was influential in the declining preeminence of the public Latin grammar school. This transplanted Old World institution had been geared toward a classical education, and its curriculum orientation underwent only slight modifications in the eighteenth century. As a result of local demands many towns did require their grammar schools to add some instruction in reading, writing, and arithmetic to their prescribed studies. Several towns also combined their grammar and elementary schools under a single master while a few other towns even used this enlarged grammar school as a moving school. Despite these alterations however, the public grammar school remained basically directed toward the classical ideal and to instruction along traditional lines. Many public grammar schools, including the venerable Boston Latin School, continued to neglect the teaching of mathematics. These schools therefore failed to satisfy the needs of a growing number of young boys who were not intent on preparing for college and who required new forms of vocational training. These youths now looked to other institutions for their requisite vocational education.

To satisfy these needs for broadened vocational education, private schools soon appeared at both the elementary and secondary levels. Most of these private schools offered a wide variety of couses in either academic or vocational categories, and some offered instruction in both areas. Private schools generally were not obliged to follow a prescribed curriculum and thus were able to keep their course offerings abreast of the times. Although some private grammar schools were established in the eighteenth century, most of them closed after a short time when their schoolmasters entered more lucrative occupations. It was the newer, utilitarian private schools that developed as the more-popular and especially more-relevant educational institution.

The private schools—particularly the vocational ones—were initially established in the larger towns. As early as 1709 in Boston Owen Harris was offering private instruction in writing, arithmetic, geometry, trigonometry, astronomy, surveying, gauging, and the use of mathematical instruments. In 1715 John Sanderline, another Boston schoolmaster, offered to teach navigation as well as writing and arithmetic. Other private teachers gave business training, and in 1727 Caleb Philips advertised instruction in shorthand. From 1730 onward, the numerous advertisements for private schools in Boston's newspapers indicated how widely these institutions flourished in the community. In New Haven and New London private schools offering a broad, practical curriculum were founded in the decade preceding the American Revolution. Newport gave private vocational training before 1750 and Providence followed with similar instruction somewhat later. Portsmouth, New Hampshire and other small towns also gave private vocational training so that by the end of this period, all the New England colonies had been at least affected by the more utilitarian forms of study.

Despite the wide variety in their curricula, New England's private schools of the later colonial period were not academies. Some of them, such as the Governor Dummer grammar school, established in South Byfield, Massachusetts in 1761, did become academies after the outbreak of the American Revolution. Others, such as Nathan Tisdale's school in Lebanon, Connecticut were referred to as academies for prestige purposes. However, the emergence of actual academies in New England, with administrative control vested in self-perpetuating or relatively independent trustees and dependent on both private and public aid, was to become prominent later in the post-Revolutionary period.

Teachers and Textbooks

The profession of schoolmaster in eighteenth-century New England continued to contain individuals of such diverse backgrounds as in the 1600s. A growing population caused an increased need for teachers, and the changing economic environment necessitated more masters knowledgeable in technical subjects, but basically minimal qualifications remained in effect. Towns still employed ill-trained individuals as teachers; Providence, for example, hired William Turpin, an innkeeper, as its first schoolmaster, while other towns used unemployed tradesmen in their schoolrooms. Salaries continued to affect the overall competence of teachers, though the teachers in grammar schools usually were better prepared than those in the elementary town or district schools. Generally, the best teaching was still done by college graduates who were awaiting a ministerial call or by those who combined preaching and teaching. In addition, some college undergraduates such as Benjamin Trumbull (Yale 1759) and Abiel Foster (Harvard 1756) kept schools during their undergraduate years. Yet, despite the increased number of college students and graduates who devoted at least part of their careers to education, the shortage of qualified teachers—especially in rural settlements—continued well beyond the colonial period.

During the eighteenth century, there were a few actions designed to regulate teacher certification more closely in some New England colonies. Massachusetts, which originally left the informal licensing of teachers to selectmen, made a new move in 1701. In that year a statute required that grammar schoolmasters should be approved "by the minister of the town and the two next adjacent towns or any two of them." During the 1760s, royal commissions to two of New Hampshire's governors included the provision that all schoolmasters in the colony were to be licensed by the governor ,and that schoolmasters coming from England must also be licensed by the Bishop of London. Both of these cases reflect attempts to discriminate among schoolmasters along sectarian lines and possibly to ensure the proper scholarly competence of teachers. Yet such actions had relatively little effect on the existing means of teacher selection in most New England communities. Town officials and school committees still possessed the principal voice in the hiring and firing of public schoolmasters though private teachers usually went unlicensed.

The later colonial period saw a variety of textbooks adopted in New England schools, but the *New England Primer* remained the most popular text. Most booksellers carried several copies of the *Primer* and during the period from 1749 to 1766 one Philadelphia firm reportedly sold 37,100 copies of the work. New and enlarged editions were printed throughout the eighteenth century. Several of these later *Primers* contained additional illustrations, poems, proverbs, or prayers while others included new rhymes to the alphabet section. Basically, however, the main approach of the *New England Primer* remained unchanged; it was a sectarian book designed to promote a sectarian education.

There were other new textbooks that appeared in New England schoolrooms at this time. One of the most notable of these books was Thomas Dilworth's *A New Guide to the English Tongue*, first published in 1740. This book, which became the most popular speller of the eighteenth century, combined spelling with religious and ethical precepts. Other less celebrated spellers or readers in use were authored by George Fisher, Daniel Fenning, Henry Dixon, and the English hymnist, Isaac Watts. Instruction in arithmetic was usually given without the assistance of textbooks although after 1750 some arithmetic texts began to appear in the schools of larger towns. Once again Thomas Dilworth authored the best work in the field. Entitled *The Schoolmaster's Assistant*, it was published first in London in 1743 and reprinted in Philadelphia in 1769. Earlier, although less prominent, texts were Edward Cocker's *Arithmetic*, James Hodder's *Arithmetic* and Isaac Greenwood's *Arithmetick, Vulgar and Decimal*. Additional works of classical authors appeared in secondary schools, but despite a growing interest in history and geography, few textbooks in these fields were in use until after the American Revolution.

Higher Education

Three new colleges were founded in New England during the later colonial period. The first of these institutions dates from 1701 when Connecticut's General Assembly chartered the Collegiate School of Connecticut. The Collegiate School was first located in Saybrook, but after some localist squabbling it was removed to New Haven in 1716 and renamed Yale College after an affluent English benefactor. During the next decade the new college had some precarious moments when its Congregationist rector unexpectedly became an Episcopalian, but under his successors the college maintained its orthodox Congregational base. By the middle of the eighteenth century, Yale College had obtained a liberal and largely autonomous charter from the colonial legislature, and in the two decades before the Revolution it generally paralleled Harvard in the size of student enrollment.

The other two new colleges were founded several years after Yale, and both were influenced by the Great Awakening as well as by the growing spirit of rationalism. The College of Rhode Island was incorporated in 1764 under the presidency of the Reverend James Manning. It also experienced localist quarrels over its ultimate site, but the school was finally settled in Providence in 1770 and renamed Brown College, after a prominent local merchant. The college's charter had quite liberal provisions including a renunciation of religious tests for admission and the opening of faculty positions to Protestants of all denominations. One year prior to Brown's settlement in Providence, the New Hampshire legislature issued a charter to Dartmouth College to be located in Hanover. Named after a prominent and humanitarian English benefactor, the college was the outgrowth of an Indian school first established after the Great Awakening in Lebanon, Connecticut by the Reverend Eleazar Wheelock. Like Brown College, Dartmouth's charter also contained liberal religious provisions, and like Brown, it also enrolled few students prior to 1775.

In college administration, Harvard continued its previous innovative practice of control through the Corporation and Overseers. The other New England colleges, however, did not follow Harvard's administrative example. Instead, they generally followed the Yale College model of government by the head of the college and a single self-perpetuating board of trustees. Since all the New England colleges had sectarian affiliations, it followed that denominational affiliation was usually related to a trustee's appointment and that most trustees were ministers. An exception was Brown College whose charter called for a multidenominational board of trustees which could include laymen.

Financial problems persisted for all college administrators throughout the colonial period. Although New England colleges often received generous benefactions, these schools were forced to rely on additional assistance from the colonial legislatures or the local community. During this period, Yale obtained several land grants plus an annual £100 grant from the General Assembly. Dartmouth was given a 44,000 acre land grant as part of its original charter. Nevertheless, college maintenance costs increased—particularly at Harvard and Yale—so that income from tuition became more extensively relied on for needed revenues.

A steady growth in the number of students added considerably to the tuition income of colleges. During the two decades preceding the Revolution, the student bodies at Harvard and Yale often surpassed 150—including several undergraduates from outside New England. Entrance examinations were still oriented toward the classics and were administered to candidates who had been privately tutored or educated in grammar schools. The age range of accepted freshmen was quite broad: Nathan Holt entered Harvard in 1753 at age 28, while John

Trumbull passed Yale's entrance examination at 7. The median age for most undergraduates, however, was about 16, and despite the continued strictness of college discipline, the students were not averse to troublemaking. At Harvard there were recurring complaints of "rude and prophane" conduct in chapel, while both Harvard and Yale experienced occasional undergraduate "riots" like this one described in the diary of a Yale College freshman:

January 16, (1756): Many of the Students of College gathered together in the evening, and rung the Bell, and fired Crackers, Run the Yard, and hollowed & Screamed in a terrible manner and several of this Riot was catch'd by the Tutors, among which Pell a Junior was Suspended from College and Burbanks in the Sophimore Class; Huntington a Sophimore Rusticated, and many others were boxed by the President.

The principal trend within New England colleges during this period was manifested in the growth of secularism and the corresponding decline in rigid sectarianism. This liberal predeliction first emerged at Harvard during the presidency of John Leverett (1707–1724), who had succeeded the Reverend Increase Mather. The more lenient atmosphere under Leverett was later broadened during the progressive administration of the Reverend Edward Holyoke (1737–1769). Yale reached its peak of orthodoxy during the stern administration of the Reverend Thomas Clap (1740–1766), but after his forced resignation, his successor, the Reverend Naphtali Daggett (1766–1777), ruled in a more moderate fashion. Brown and Dartmouth were founded shortly before the Revolution, but even so, evidence of this secular trend was quite noticeable at both institutions.

Manifestations of this secular spirit were apparent in the broadening curricula of the colleges. In 1722 Harvard established a professorship of mathematics and natural philosphy—the first in a secular subject. Under its initial holders, John Winthrop IV and Isaac Greenwood, interest in these studies expanded so that, by 1760, scientific subjects in the curriculum accounted for at least one-fifth of a student's classroom time. Readings from Newton, Locke, and other luminaries of the Enlightenment entered other studies, and for a brief period Harvard employed a French instructor. Yale was also affected by the new learning. Works of the European Enlightenment, particularly in science and mathematics, were pondered even during the austere administration of President Clap. During his successor's rule, the college finally gained its own professorship of mathematics and natural philosophy.

There were other signs of growing secularism in New England's higher education. While the most popular single career for graduates remained theology, an ever-increasing number were turning toward law, medicine, trade, or commerce. Richard Hofstadter, who noted that 52 percent of Harvard's seventeenth-century graduates entered the ministry, also noted that the number dropped to below 40 percent among the classes graduating during the final decades of the colonial period. Yale showed a somewhat similar trend. Undoubtedly, the rising interest in Enlightenment studies contributed to this worldly outlook, yet at the same time, the new learning was also preparing a more aware and broadly educated college graduate. Student disputations, which now included such temporal topics as "Does Civil Government originate from compact?," and, "Are the People the Sole Judge of their Rights and Liberties?" were reflections of this new consciousness among students. In New England, colleges were steadily becoming centers of independence, vitality, and social usefulness. This fact was significantly exemplified by a member of the Harvard Corporation who observed, in the early 1770s, that "the young gentlemen are taken up with politics—They have caught the spirit of liberty."

Girls' Education

The restrictive seventeenth-century attitudes toward female education continued throughout the later colonial period. Most New England women remained unaffected by the societal changes of the eighteenth century. It was still deemed necessary that young girls should be imbued with a knowledge of the Scriptures and be taught the necessaries for being a good wife, but because of a woman's subordinate role in society there seemed little to add to this limited foundation. Formal education for the typical middle-class girl still concluded at the elementary level, and usually consisted of reading, writing, and possibly sewing or basic arithmetic. Many town or district schools educated boys and girls together, but other towns provided separate education for both sexes. There were very few moves to alter these existing patterns. At a Yale College commencement in 1773, Nathan Hale, then a graduating senior, successfully affirmed the proposition, "Whether the Education of Daughters be without any just reason more neglected than that of our Sons?." Girls, however, continued to be barred from New England's colleges as well as its public grammar schools.

There were some deviations from previously established principles for girls' education. In Massachusetts for instance, a 1710 revision of previous apprenticeship statutes included the stipulation that only males were to be taught to read and write and "females to read as they respectively may be capable." The adverse effect of this amendatory statute was reflected by one educational historian who estimated that only 40 percent of the women in eighteenth century Massachusetts could write their own signatures.

One facet of learning that did present broadened opportunities for some girls lay in the realm of private education. During the later colonial period, a growing number of private schools and private tutors appeared, catering primarily to the desires of the growing number of affluent families of the "better sort." Some private schools were coeducational while others were for girls only. The private girls' schools were established in the larger towns and they generally offered a wider curriculum than did their counterparts of the seventeenth century. Girls schools in Boston, Newport, Salem, and other towns offered such diverse subjects as reading, writing, arithmetic, embroidery, music, French, painting, dancing, millinery, and sewing. Despite the varied nature of such course offerings, the total educational opportunities for females still fell short of those open to boys. A privileged girl's education might stress the utilitarian subjects and the social frills, but it did not advance beyond fundamentals in subjects such as mathematics, and overall it offered little of real intellectual value.

Indian and Negro Education

Most of New England's original settlers had initially looked upon the region's Indian inhabitants with sincere benevolence. In fact, the early Puritan immigrants regarded these natives as descendants of one of the lost tribes of Israel. They therefore sought to remold the Indians into their own image of civilized living. Missionaries, such as the Reverends Thomas Mayhew and John Eliot, labored to spread the gospel and to convert the Indians as soon as possible. Eliot himself published in 1663 an Algonquin version of the Bible that was distributed among the estimated 4000 converted, or "praying," Indians who settled in Puritan towns. By the end of the seventeenth century, however, the early missionary endeavors had largely collapsed. Too often the energetic Puritan attempts at remaking and converting the Indians had been undone by patronizing, self-righteous and inflexible attitudes that led to aggressive hostility and bloody warfare. During the following century, the earlier missionary fervor subsided and the contempt and animosity toward the Indians was reflected by Cotton Mather who dismissed them as "pernicious creatures."

The extent of Indian education during the colonial period was directly related to these developments. Converting the Indian to Christianity automatically meant instructing him at least in reading. One effective group formed in 1649 to promote these joint educational-missionary aims was "The Society for the Propagation of the Gospel in New England." Through the efforts of this society and individual missionaries, schools were established in the "Praying Indian" towns, while in other communities town and grammar schools were opened to Indian children. Massachusetts Bay made the most extensive endeavors for formal education of the natives, but other colonies, such as Connecticut and Plymouth, also made significant efforts against their illiteracy. A few Indians were even exposed to higher education during the seventeenth century. An Indian College, with its own separate building was established at Harvard during the 1650s, and about seven or eight Indian boys were introduced to the undergraduate curriculum. Only one of them, however (Caleb Cheeshateaumuck, class of 1665) graduated from the college. By the close of the century, however, these notable educational efforts had waned along with the efforts toward religious conversion.

During the eighteenth century, there was no widespread attempt to recreate the earlier forms of missionary education for Indians. It is true that sects such as the Moravians and Episcopalians promoted religious learning, and that during the Great Awakening some evangelical Calvinists also gave instruction among various tribes. Nevertheless, the social and economic changes in the new century, as well as the removal of most Indians to the frontier, had served to alter the aims and scope of missionary education. Even Dartmouth College, which was an outgrowth of the Great Awakening's missionary zeal, enrolled few Indian students before or after the American Revolution.

The number of Negroes in colonial New England was relatively small. The first Negro in New England apparently came to Plymouth Colony in the late 1620s while the first group of Negroes was brought to Massachusetts Bay in 1638. Subsequently, however, there was no large influx of Negroes since the region proved unconducive to widespread chattel slavery. In 1700 there were probably less than 1000 Negroes in all New England, with over half that number living in Massachusetts. By the eve of the American Revolution, their number was listed as 16,034 out of a total population of 659,446. Partly because of this small number, chattel slavery was probably less repressive here than elsewhere in colonial America, and a substantial number of the Negro slaves in the region attained their freedom.

The education of Negroes in New England was influenced by these previously mentioned factors. Although they were subjected to discriminatory laws, particularly during the later colonial period, Negroes were granted a considerable degree of legal equality and were never completely excluded from sharing in the social and economic activities of whites. Thus, there were never any statutes in New England colonies forbidding the instruction of slaves, and black children were apparently included within the scope of compulsory education laws. Indeed, many masters found it economically advantageous to educate their slaves. A study by Lorenzo J. Greene concluded that because of economic considerations, "many of the New England Negroes received elementary instruction in writing, reading, and arithmetic, as well as industrial training." While such learning opportunities existed at the elementary level, no Negro attended any of the colleges in the region, and apparently few, if any, were enrolled in grammar schools.

Efforts to educate Negroes as a distinct group came principally in the realm of religion. The Reverend John Eliot first advocated sectarian education for blacks, and in 1717 Cotton Mather opened a short-lived evening charity school for Indians and Negroes. The efforts of Mather and other ministers marked the beginning of a period during which a rising number of Negroes were being converted and accepted as members of Congregational Churches. Missionary endeavors by other denominations were also made during the later colonial period. The Episcopalians in particular encouraged their missionaries to found schools specifically for sectarian instruction.

*　　*　　*

During the prerevolutionary years of the eighteenth century, New England's educational patterns had undergone considerable broadening and diversification. The results had reflected not only a growing divergence from customary European modes of education, but also a response to particular American conditions. The widespread economic, social, religious, and intellectual developments in eighteenth-century New England necessitated educational changes and the region's schools had altered their earlier forms to meet these new needs. Examples of such changes, as cited in this chapter, occurred at all educational levels, though they were especially evident in the increasing number of private secondary-level vocational training schools. Changes were also reflected by a remarkable improvement in the general level of writing and spelling from seventeenth-century standards. The drift from earlier learning practices was becoming more pronounced. While New Englanders ended the colonial period still devoted to many of their seventeenth-century educational traditions, they were simultaneously transforming their educational structure to meet the specific needs of their rapidly changing society.

chapter four
education in the southern colonies, 1607-1776

The individuals who settled the lands from Chesapeake Bay southward through Georgia resembled their New England counterparts in some ways and differed from them in others. There were numerous examples of such parallels and contrasts. The majority of settlers who emigrated to New England and to the southern colonies were Englishmen and, in both regions, they endeavored to preserve many of the same English customs, traditions, and political institutions; and in both regions many individuals strove to keep abreast of Old World cultural and intellectual developments. Yet the inhabitants of these two sections also had their differences. While religious dissent had been the principal motivating force behind the exodus to New England, economic impulses chiefly underlay the settlement of the South. Also, New Englanders had originally migrated on a group or family basis from the middle levels of English society. The southern settlers, on the other hand, arrived on an individual footing from more diverse social backgrounds. Geographic and climatic variances between the two regions led to even wider sectional and individual differences by the end of the colonial period.

Southern educational patterns also contained parallels and

divergences from those of New England. Both sections looked to English models in establishing their initial systems of learning. Both sections also attempted to adjust educational practices to their particular social and economic needs. Southerners, however, did not share the same characteristics of dissent against the English establishment that had marked the Puritan migrations to New England. As a result, the prevailing educational principles of the southern colonies came much closer to those of the mother country than did New England's.

The highly individualistic and class-oriented educational features that the South transplanted from England illustrated their affinity to the social system of the mother country. In 1671 Governor Sir William Berkeley of Virginia clearly noted this transplantation. When asked about the nature of education in his colony, he replied succinctly: "The same course that is taken in England out of towns; every man according to his own ability in instructing his children."

The Settlement and Administration of the Southern Colonies

In 1607, Virginia became the first southern colony with the founding of Jamestown. The settlement was the result of mercantile efforts by London merchants who were members of the joint stock Virginia Company. Virginia, however, paid none of the expected dividends to its profit-minded stockholders, and, in fact, it was almost abandoned on several occasions during its first decade of existence. Although tobacco growing eventually gave the settlers a basis for permanence, the company was unable to maintain its solvency and stability. Finally, in 1625 Virginia became a royal colony under the control of a crown-appointed governor. This royal colony status was retained for over 150 years, during which time Virginia remained the most populous and prestigious of all southern colonies.

Maryland, Virginia's adjoining Chesapeake colony, was founded in 1633. Unlike its neighbor, Maryland was established as a proprietary colony under a royal grant given to George Calvert (Lord Baltimore) and his heirs. The Calverts hoped to gain riches from their grant and at the same time provide a religious haven for their fellow Roman Catholics. Few riches were forthcoming, however, and the immigration of more Protestants than Catholics to the colony increased the opposition to strong proprietary control. After one antiproprietor revolt in 1689, Maryland became a royal colony for 24 years. The proprietorship was restored after the Calverts' reconversion to Protestantism, but the family was never able to reassert much authority over the inhabitants. Maryland's population and size always remained less than Virginia's.

The Carolinas originated from a proprietary grant given by Charles II in 1663 to eight royal favorites. Although these proprietors also dreamed of wealth and even approved a grandiose governmental scheme for the inhabitants, their direct involvement in the affairs of the region was limited. The Carolinas, consequently, each developed in its own particular way. North Carolina became a colony that consisted primarily of small, scattered farms with no real urban centers. South Carolina, on the other hand, developed an extensive plantation system that radiated outward from Charleston, the largest town in the colonial South. Ultimately, proprietary control over both Carolinas collapsed, and both became royal colonies, South Carolina in 1721 and North Carolina in 1729.

Georgia, the last and least populated southern colony, was not settled until 1733. Its genesis lay in both the royal government's desires to provide a buffer between the Carolinas and Spanish Florida and the proposals of certain British philanthropists to provide a haven for formerly imprisoned debtors. A 21-year charter was granted to these philanthropists under a trusteeship in 1732, and the first settlement was made at Savannah the following year. Yet, despite idealistic attempts to limit landholdings and forbid slavery, a slave-based plantation system soon emerged. In 1752 the trustees acknowledged their failures by surrendering their charter to the royal government.

The pattern of royal administration and control was explicit in almost all southern colonies. It explained part of the strong attachments southern colonists had with England, attachments that caused their attempt to emulate the mother country in so many societal aspects. Other facets of life in the colonial South reveal similar examples of these tendencies.

Religious and Social Patterns in the Colonial South

Outwardly the religious structure of the southern colonies showed a strong affinity to England. The Episcopal church was one of the institutions transferred to Virginia by its original settlers. In 1611 it was recognized as the colony's established church. Eight years later Virginia's first General Assembly meeting enacted legislation providing for the legal establishment of the Church of England, and the colony's royal government passed subsequent acts consolidating this establishment. Other southern colonies passed similar bills under the influence of the royal government. By 1758 the Episcopal church was legally established to varying degrees throughout the South. Dissenter sects did become more numerous and active during the eighteenth century—particularly in the backcountry areas. The South nevertheless remained an Anglican stronghold until the American Revolution.

Despite its privileged position, the Church of England failed to emerge as a powerful force throughout the region. Several factors were responsible for this paradoxical situation. Foremost was a continual shortage of Episcopal priests who had to be ordained in England and who were usually unenthusiastic about coming to America. North Carolina, for example, had no Anglican clergyman until 1700, while Virginia in 1702 had 45 parishes but only 34 Episcopal priests. In addition, the poor quality of many Episcopal clergymen who did come to the South weakened the church's influence. Several southern governors criticized the competence of these clergymen, and, in 1696, one Virginia rector complained to the Bishop of London:

"Several ministers have caused such high scandals of late and have raised such prejudices amongst the people against the clergy, that hardly can they be persuaded to take a clergyman into their parish." The absence of a resident bishop made it difficult to discipline such backsliders or adequately regulate church affairs. Church commissaries were sent by the Bishop of London to represent him in America, but their actual powers proved limited. As a result of this lack of effective hierarchical control, the vestries of most southern parishes administered their own churches largely on an independent and often informal basis.

The distribution of population in the southern colonies was still another factor restricting both religious and intellectual vitality. With the evolution of large plantations, many parishes extended over 100 square miles. Consequently, the location of the parish church caused most rural families to travel considerable distances to attend services. Many Southerners neglected their church attendance and only a minority of them were regular communicants. In fact, both North Carolina and Georgia had few Episcopal churches before the Revolution. Unlike New England, therefore, southern churches failed to become primary centers of spiritual or intellectual activity.

Probably the most notable aspects in the South's spiritual surroundings were made through the endeavors of The Society for the Propagation of the Gospel in Foreign Parts. Organized in England in 1701 as an auxiliary of the Episcopal Church, the principal purpose of the Society was to perform missionary work among Indians and Negroes in English colonies. It was also expected to provide for the spiritual needs of white settlers who lacked Episcopal churches or priests. Much of the Society's efforts in these directions focused on the American colonies, where 300 missionaries and over 20 schoolmasters were sent from 1702 to 1785. Many of these men were assigned to the southern colonies where they generally labored with energy, enthusiasm, and devotion to the Episcopal cause. Overcoming hardships and often opposition, they ministered to scattered communicants, sought new converts, founded churches, distributed Bibles and prayer books, and established libraries. Their educational activities were part of this same program. Yet, despite their efforts and successes, particularly in South Carolina, the S.P.G. was unable to bring religion to a foremost position within the southern social order.

The social structure of the region was determined largely by the characteristics of its original settlers. Unlike Plymouth and Massachusetts Bay, Virginia's earliest immigrants arrived on an individual basis and represented a wide range of England's social hierarchy. The upper extreme consisted of a small group of leaders in the Jamestown settlement who had come from the higher levels of English society. They included the sons of earls, lords, privy councillors, and the higher clergy. Although most of this early Virginia ruling elite failed to survive the first generation of settlement, they did succeed in transplanting the English concept of rule through an aristocratic landed gentry. At the opposite end of the social scale were the majority of immigrants who were from the lower English social orders and who came to Virginia as servants. They included unemployed workers, vagrants, indigent or orphaned children, and even convicts who were persuaded or coerced into sailing to America as servants. The need for servile laborers continually increased and their growing numbers in Virginia aided the tendencies to deliniate the settlers into social classes along English lines. Somewhat similar factors also affected the social composition of other southern colonies.

Despite the efforts of its leaders, southern society did not become a carbon copy of England's ordered class structure. Economic, environmental, and other factors hindered the complete attainment of this goal. Nonetheless, the colonial South did achieve significant similarities to English class models, and these similarities were distinctly reflected in fields such as education. The southern class structure of the later colonial period exemplified this phenomenon.

At its uppermost level the southern social order was represented by the great planter families. They had reached their prominent positions either as a result of personal struggles as original pioneers or, like the Byrd and Carter families of Virginia, as the immigrant younger sons of affluent English families. Whatever their origins, these families eventually perpetuated the earlier ideals of a ruling elite. This southern aristocracy was particularly prominent in Maryland, Virginia, and South Carolina, and as the late Arthur M. Schlesinger pointed out, it attained "a close resemblance to England's landed gentry." On their extensive estates these plantation gentry constantly strove to emulate the customs, dress, and habits of English rural squires. The plantation's manor house thus became the center of rural southern social activity. In the region's few significant towns, such as Charleston, Baltimore, and Norfolk, some resident merchants were also included among the social elite but their number was comparatively small.

Those who comprised the middle levels of southern society generally lacked the prestige of their counterparts in the other colonial sections. Most of these individuals were small, independent farmers, scattered throughout North Carolina, Georgia, and the interior sections of South Carolina, Maryland, and Virginia. Despite their landowning status these yeomen farmers were usually superseded by the planter aristocracy. Free white plantation workers and a small number of artisans and tradesmen in the few urban centers constituted the remainder of this subordinate middle class.

Indentured servants composed the base of the white southern social structure. These indentured servants were men and women who had made a contract or indenture that obligated them to labor for a colonial master in return for food, clothing, shelter, and transportation to America. Charles M. Andrews has estimated that three quarters of those settlers who came to Virginia before 1642 were indentured, and an almost equally large proportion of indentured servants came to Maryland during its early years of settlement. The term of indenture was generally from four to seven years, but upon its expiration the servant became a free person. As in other colonies, indentures were used for various occupations, although agriculture became the principal outlet for such labor in the South. The practice continued in America well beyond the Revolution, but by the eighteenth century it was already being overshadowed by the system of chattel slavery.

The institution of chattel slavery brought forth a distinct social category in the region. The first Negroes were sold into servitude in Virginia in 1619 although it was not until after the middle of the century that their numbers increased to any considerable degree. At first, many of them may have been like white servants and released after a term of service. It soon became evident, however, that Negroes offered the ambitious planter greater opportunities for profit and a cheaper solution to his labor needs. These facts, combined with the Negroes' distinctive racial characteristics, inexorably led to fixing upon black men the well-defined status of chattel. Though unrecognized by English law, this status differentiated Negroes from other servants and forced them into lifetime servitude. It also relegated the Negro into a debased societal position in which he was deprived of most rights granted to whites. Nevertheless, chattel slavery became widely accepted, especially among the planter aristocrats, and by the end of the colonial period the South had far more Negroes held in bondage than had the other colonial sections.

Economic Life in the Southern Colonies

Economic patterns of life in the colonial South, like social practices, had their origins in the early years of settlement. The first settlers who came to Virginia were unable to find their anticipated riches in gold and silver. They were also unable to establish a compact, trading-post system of settlement that relied on the local natives to furnish their food supply. After abortive attempts to produce wines, iron, silk, and other commodities, the colonists turned to the native tobacco plant in order to stabilize their economic existence.

Because of several factors, the cultivation of tobacco almost inevitably led to the development of large plantations. One such factor lay in the rapidly increasing European market for this commodity. (Virginia tobacco production jumped from 20,000 pounds in 1617 to 40 million pounds by 1700.) Farmers needed more lands not only to satisfy increased production demands but also to replace the soil exhausted from growing tobacco. Unlike New England, the fertile tidewater areas of Chesapeake Bay offered such extensive lands for large-scale farming. The headright system, under which generous land grants were made to certain settlers, directly promoted the expansion of this type of agriculture. Later, with the available supply of cheap slave labor, the large planters were further motivated to increase their landholdings. The plantation system finally emerged, therefore, and dominated the tobacco lands of Maryland and the rice and indigo fields of South Carolina.

Plantations were generally large, self-contained economic units. Their size varied from several hundred to several thousand acres, and they usually had a frontage on a navigable river. The center of the plantation was the great house where the planter and his family lived. Surrounding the house were the workhouses in which the cooking, baking, weaving, blacksmithing, and repair work were done. Farther away were the barns and dwellings for the servants and slaves. Most of the plantation's foodstuffs were produced upon it, as was clothing and other necessary articles. Since the plantation had its own resident labor force and a river access to ocean-going ships, it required little assistance from its neighbors. Items that could not be manufactured on the plantation were usually imported directly from England.

The large planter was not isolated from the outside world. His economic ties to his neighboring planters were often reflected in the debts they owed to the same English merchants. In politics, the large planters frequently dominated the colonial assemblies, and other ties were formed through social gatherings and family marriages. Education, particularly at the higher levels, also served as a mixing ground for the sons of the plantation aristocracy.

Not all of the South's lands were divided into large plantations, however. In fact, Thomas J. Wertenbaker has noted that as late as 1700 Virginia was still a colony filled primarily "with little farms a few hundred acres in extent, owned and worked by a sturdy class of English farmers." By the end of the colonial era, most of these small farmers were living in the interior lands of Virginia and Maryland and the backwoods of South Carolina. In North Carolina and Georgia they were scattered throughout all sections of the colony. These small, independent farmers labored with difficulty to eke out a subsistence living. In some cases they rented their lands from the plantation aristocracy and, often in selling their produce, they were dominated by this same gentry. Although these factors created sharper class distinctions than in New England, the voting powers of the smaller farmers helped prevent an exact transplantation of the English brand of economic aristocracy.

The southern agricultural system naturally prevented the development of large urban centers. Charleston was the only community that could be called a city. Baltimore, Norfolk, and Richmond grew to the level of small towns, while Annapolis and Williamsburg remained little more than large villages. It is true that these settlements did represent varying outlets for economic, social, and intellectual activity. Yet the South still remained far more rural than urban throughout the entire colonial period.

Education and Life in the Colonial South

Several factors influencing education emerge from this survey of life in the southern colonies. One was the South's vigorous attempts to reproduce prevailing English institutions as closely as possible within their society. These efforts were visible in various aspects, including the adoption of English governmental models, the establishment of the Anglican Church, and the endeavors to create a rural gentry in the Chesapeake tidewater and South Carolina farmlands. In much the same way, educational aims and practices were also reminiscent of those in the mother country. Southerners, while concerned about learning, accepted the existing English precept that education was primarily a private rather than a public matter. Unlike New England, the South did not regard education as a means of building a new social order and enacted no legislation requiring local governments to establish schools or to legalize their support through taxation. This acceptance and emulation of England's educational legacy was especially pronounced among the South's planter aristocracy. Their attempts to imitate the education offered to children of English country squires became a hallmark of southern schooling even beyond the American Revolution.

There were several other deterrents to an advanced system of public schooling in the South. One of the most obvious of these deterrents was the South's dispersed agrarian pattern of settlement. The effects of the absence of community life were noted by one Virginia clergyman who wrote in 1662 that "from their sparse population has resulted their almost general want of Schooles, for the education of their Children, is another consequent of their scattered planting, of most sad consideration, most of all bewailed of Parents there . . . ." Another deterrent was the general absence of a strong religious interest in promoting knowledge. With a few exceptions, most Episcopalians lacked the Puritans' theological emphasis on a system of mandatory, state-supported schools. A third hindrance against the developing of a public school system in the South was the sharply ordered class structure. Planter aristocrats, who were quite capable of privately educating their own children, had no desire to endanger their predominant class position by promoting a system of popular schooling. And they were especially fearful of the danger of educating their slave population.

The effects of these factors were clearly defined. Although southern families shared the same Puritan fear that their children would be corrupted by the wilderness environment, their attitudes, institutions, and living patterns prevented them from attaining New England's progressive educational achievements. The result was that education in the South, as in England, became primarily an individual matter. It was up to most white parents alone to educate or not to educate their children as the opportunties presented themselves. In addition, the particular needs of the region caused many Southerners to reconsider their educational expectations. Thus, the Reverend James Maury, writing to a friend in 1762, asserted that the English upperclass training in the classics was unnecessary for the education of a Virginia gentleman:

It long has been, and still is, Matter of Doubt with me whether the Study of the Grecian & Roman Tongues be (I do not say necessary, for it seems quite obvious it is not, but even) proper for all your Youth, who are sent to a Grammar-school, who have Genius equal to the Task, & the Circumstances of whose Parents bid fair for placing them above manual Labor & servile Employments, after their Attainment to Manhood. In the Instances above-mentioned [i.e., in England], indeed, the propriety & even Necessity, of these Studies, are undeniable; but in this Case, which involves almost all our Youth above the lower Ranks in this Quarter of the World, I am far from convinced, that they are necessary or proper.

Most recent educational historians, particularly Edgar W. Knight, Lawrence Cremin, and Louis Wright, have acknowledged these determining influences on southern education. Their studies offer excellent insights into the South's educational hindrances as well as the representative features of its learning system. As in the case of New England, this southern learning system can be divided into both informal and formal categories.

Informal Educational Patterns

Family life, where informal education initially centered, developed more slowly in the South than in New England. As previously noted, the earliest settlers in Virginia and Maryland migrated primarily on an individual, rather than a family basis. The fact that women did not arrive in Virginia in any significant numbers until 1619 delayed the beginnings of family life until well into the second decade after the founding of Jamestown. Even after the planters selected their brides from among the young women sent to them, the continued existence of a large servant class among the Chesapeake settlers impeded the establishment of family patterns such as those in New England. The situation in Virginia and Maryland was later repeated to varying extents within other southern colonies.

Nevertheless, the family groups eventually emerged in the South. As in New England, the family was expected to provide children with their initial moral and religious training. Families in the South, however, were on a more dispersed footing than the more close-knit New Englanders. As a result, individual southern families were often faced with the task of providing for extended education by themselves alone. A number of small planters and backwoods farmers, without any legal compulsion, took time out from their arduous labors to instruct their children in reading and sometimes writing. A few children, such as Patrick Henry, even had the exceptional privilege of a college-educated father as their tutor. Yet most of the children of the less-affluent white southerners were not even fortunate enough to receive the basic rudiments of a literate education in their information instruction. Consequently, they grew up to be as unaware of book learning as their own parents.

Aside from parental training, the principal type of informal education in the region centered around the apprenticeship system. As in New England, the basic features of the southern apprenticeship system were inherited from England and had an admixture of economic, religious, and humanitarian aims. Also, as in New England, the apprenticeship system formed the principal means of informal training for a child's future vocational career. In some southern colonies the presence of numerous indigent and dependent white children resulted in a much broader educational scope to their apprenticeship system.

Virginia, of all the southern colonies, attained the most complete provisions for education through apprenticeship, and was the first to enact apprenticeship legislation. The need for such legislation became evident soon after the colony had gained economic stability. Indentured servitude, which satisfied the earliest needs of Virginia tobacco farmers, also brought with it the growth of special classes of dependent children. These groups consisted largely of children of indentured servants, illegitimate and indigent children, and orphaned children who began arriving in significant numbers in 1619. For all these children the family unit either did not exist or was unable to provide for any of their education. Virginians, like New Englanders, felt that such "barberous" and "stubborn" children formed a serious threat to their society. They also felt it incumbent upon the state to provide a means of harnessing the labor of these children in a disciplined and beneficial manner. In 1642, therefore, Virginia's General Assembly, clearly copying existing English laws, adopted its first apprenticeship statute:

Whereas sundry laws and statutes by act of parliament established, have with great wisdom ordained, for the better educateing of youth in honest and profitable trades and manufactures, as also to avoyd sloath and idlnesse wherewith such young children are easily corrupted, as also for reliefe of such parents whose poverty extends not to give them breeding. That the justices of the peace should at their discretion, bind out children to tradesmen or husbandmen to be brought vp in some good and lawfull calling. And whereas God Almighty, among many his other blessings, hath vouchsafed increase of children to this collony, who now are multiplied to a considerable number, who is instructed in good and lawfull trades may much improve the honor and reputation of the country, and noe lesse their owne good and theire parents comfort: But forasmuch as for the most part of the parents, either through fond indulgence or perverse obstinacy, are most averse and unwilling to parte with theire children, Be it therefore inacted by authoritie of this Grand Assembly, *according to the aforesayd laudable custom in the kingdom of England. That the commissioners of the severall countyes respectively do, at theire discretion, make choice of two children in each county of the age of eight or seaven years at the least, either male or female, which are to be sent vp to James Citty between this and June next to be imployed in the public flax houses vnder such master and mistresse as shall be there appointed, In carding, knitting, and spinning, &c. And that the said children be furnished from the said county with six barrels of corne, two coverletts, or one rugg and one blankett: One bed, one wooden bowle or tray, two pewter spoones, a sow shote of ——— months old, two laying hens, with convenient apparell both linen and woollen, with hose and shoes, And for the better provision of howseing for the said children,* It is inacted, *That there be two houses built by the first of April next of forty foot long a peece with good and substantial timber, The houses to be twenty foot broad apeece, eight foot high in the porche and a stack of brick chimneys standing in the midst of each house, and that they be lofted with sawne boardes and made with convenient partitions, And it is further thought fitt that the commissioners have caution not to take vp any children but from such parents who by reason of their poverty are disabled to maintaine and educate them.* Be it likewise agreed, *That the Governor hath agreed with the Assembly for the sume of 10000 lb. of tob'o. to be paid him the next crop, to build and finish the said howses in manner and form before expressed.*

Virginia's apprenticeship statute of 1642 fell short of the advanced educational law enacted the same year by the Massachusetts General Court. Although both laws reflected responses to economic needs and social fears, the Virginia statute failed to encompass more than these immediate exigencies within its provisions. Unlike the Massachusetts statute, there were no stipulations that those apprenticed by government officials must be taught reading, religion, or the "capital laws" of the colony. In addition, the Virginia law dealt merely with special classes of dependent children—not all colony children. There were no requirements upon officials to see that all parents and masters offered the proper vocational training and a minimum of basic education. Edgar Knight's *Documentary History of Southern Education* lists numerous seventeenth-century individual apprenticeships that obligated masters to offer their wards instruction in reading and religion as well as vocational training. The execution of such general written apprenticeships were always a matter between the master, the apprentice, and, in case of disputes, the local courts. Consequently, Virginia failed to match Massachusetts Bay's far-reaching educational provisions, although after 1642 it gradually moved to broaden the training opportunities for many of its poor and dependent children.

Several such moves occurred during the remainder of the seventeenth century. In 1643 the Virginia Assembly "enjoyned" the overseers and guardians of orphans to "educate and instruct them according to their best endeavors in Christian religion and in the rudiments of learning." Three years later the Assembly passed another act that spelled out apprenticeship procedures more specifically and provided a specific grant for a workhouse school at Jamestown. In 1656 another statute dealing with orphaned children provided that those without sufficient estates should be apprenticed and "educated according as their estates will beare." By Virginia's legal code of 1661-1662, parish vestries were given authority over the care and apprenticeship of their orphaned, illegitimate, and poor children. Then, in 1668, the Assembly empowered these vestries as well as individual counties to establish their own workhouse schools. This law was followed by an act in 1672 allowing justices and county courts to apprentice poor children in substantially the same manner as provided in England's Poor Law of 1601. Like the English law, this act failed to require any book education for those children who were apprenticed.

During the eighteenth century, Virginia enacted laws which did provide basic education for many apprenticed children. Most of these acts—as pointed out by Marcus Jernegan—dealt with compulsory education for orphaned children, although some statutes involved other dependent children. In 1705, masters of male orphaned apprentices were obliged to teach them to read and write, and, in 1727, the obligation was extended to poor boys apprenticed. Orphaned apprenticed females and poor apprenticed females did not obtain the same rights until 1751. Later, in 1769, another statute provided for the apprenticing of illegitimate children of free white women with the proviso that such children be taught to read and write. During this same period the Virginia Assembly enacted a number of statutes for enforcing these laws, including an act of 1748 that was similar to the Massachusetts law of 1642. It allowed county courts to apprentice children who were not being brought up and supported properly or whose parents neglected to take due care of their education.

The overall meaning of these later Virginia laws relating to apprentices, however, should not be misjudged. The state recognized its responsibility for the education of dependent white children but did not establish a compulsory system of education for all children. In fact, in some parishes these laws only applied to a small number of children. Similarly, while these laws were mandatory and generally included some enforcement provisions, the quality and length of education actually offered to the apprentice was restricted. Yet, despite their limitations, these statutes were not meaningless. In Virginia they had resulted in at least a limited system of compulsory education and, during the eighteenth century, the colony had approximated the educational provisions of corresponding apprenticeship laws in New England.

None of the other southern colonies enacted apprenticeship legislation as extensive as Virginia's. In 1663 a Maryland act stated that orphans with a sufficient estate were to get an education while the others were to be apprenticed. A statute of 1715 required justices to inquire annually "whether apprentices be taught their trade" and empowered these officials to remove apprentices from negligent masters. North Carolina failed to enact apprenticeship legislation. In 1715, however, a colony law provided that destitute orphans should be bound out to someone to teach them to read and write. A later statute of 1755 provided that masters of all orphaned white children should teach them to read and write. Five years later the law was broadened to include illegitimate white children.

South Carolina and Georgia probably made the least provisions for apprenticeship during this period. One South Carolina statute (1695) permitted the apprenticing of poor children, but it was not followed by legislation requiring education through apprenticeship. Georgia, settled long after the other southern colonies, did not initiate its apprenticeship laws until after the close of the colonial period. In both colonies, however, children were bound out, and the apprenticeship system was used as a means of vocational training.

Elementary Education

Southern colonial governments were largely indifferent toward the establishment of formal educational institution. As in the matter of compulsory education legislation, the Assemblies generally considered their authority limited and allowed officials or individuals to decide the extent of actual schooling. In the South the parish was the local governmental unit that nominally administered this task. However unlike their English model, and unlike New England towns, southern parishes were usually restricted in their community enterprises because of the widely scattered nature of their population. Most of them also ignored the task of establishing schools and left the initiative to the parish inhabitants themselves or to interested religious groups. Such official disinterest inevitably narrowed the availability of elementary schooling.

A few noteworthy efforts to establish elementary instruction were nevertheless made by the governments of the colonial South. The first such attempt came in 1619 when the Virginia Company endorsed an unsuccessful plan for an Indian school at Henrico. Three years later, on the recommendation of the Reverend Patrick Copland, the company agreed to support a proposed "East India" school for white children, but this scheme also failed. Maryland, in 1694, passed an act for "the Encouragement of Learning and the Advancement of Natives of this Province," but 20 years later a clergyman complained to the governor: "The case of schools is very bad . . . . What we have are insufficient." Although another act (1724) provided for the establishment of county-supervised schools where poor children would be taught free, only a few of those schools actually established survived to the Revolution. A North Carolina statute of 1745 supported the construction of a school-house at Edenton but it was not built. Funds appropriated later (1754) for building schools were diverted to support the French and Indian War, but in 1766 the colony legislature did approve the use of liquor taxes to finance a school-building at Newbern. A South Carolina statute of 1712 allowed the vestry of each parish in the colony to receive up to £12 for constructing a schoolhouse and £10 annually to support a teacher. Ten years later another act permitted certain county officials to buy lands, build schoolhouses, and levy taxes for their support. Few schools, however, resulted from this encouraging legislation. In Georgia there were no significant legislative attempts to support the establishment of schools.

The circumscribed extent of elementary education was the eventual consequence of this general inaction. Southern colonies copied the English concept of a "public" school and did not envisage tuitionless schools open to all. Only a limited number of poor white children were considered eligible for a free education; for those more-affluent children schooling was a matter usaully determined by the parents. The various forms of elementary education—endowed (free) schools, charity schools, denominational schools, old field schools, private venture schools, and private tutoring—reflected this southern social characteristic.

Endowed or free schools appeared relatively early in Virginia despite Governor Berkeley's assertion (1671) that there were "no free schools" in the colony. The first of these schools originated from the estate of a planter, Benjamin Symes, who in 1635 had willed 200 acres of land and eight milk cows to endow a free school in Elizabeth City Parish. Following the custom in England this endowed school was expected to charge tuition but at the same time, to allow a certain number of poor boys a free education. The Symes school did not open until the next decade, but in 1649, one observer found it operating with "a fine house upon it." A decade later, another free school, also located in Elizabeth City Parish, was endowed through the sizable legacy of Dr. Thomas Eaton. The subsequent growth of these schools, was slow, however, and, as Jernegan has noted, "hardly half a dozen of the so-called endowed free schools were in operation at any one time in the seventeenth century." A report in 1724 to the Bishop of London listed only five endowed schools in Virginia, and apparently only four more were established by the Revolution.

There were also endowed free schools in other southern colonies. In Maryland, King William's School at Annapolis appears to have been the only noteworthy endowed free school established in the colony. In South Carolina, legislative assistance in 1710 and 1712 helped lead to the founding of a free school in Charleston. Sizable bequests from affluent planters led to the founding of other free schools in the colony including the noted Winyaw Indigo Society School at Georgetown, opened in 1756. In North Carolina, the only school that might be considered a free school was the one established at Newbern in 1766. Georgia's trustees received numerous gifts for educational purposes, but no free schools were established during the colonial period.

Charity schools in the South as well as in other colonial sections were established primarily through the efforts of the Society for the Propagation of the Gospel in Foreign Parts. In line with one main objective of the Society, these charity schools were expected to emphasize Episcopal religious tenets, although most schools also offered instruction in reading, writing, and basic arithmetic. The schools were taught by the Society's missionaries or appointed schoolmasters, and despite obstacles and occasional opposition, they operated in most southern colonies. Their students, with few exceptions, came from the poorer white groups and, in several areas, charity schools offered the only education available to the lower classes. In Georgia, the charity orphan school opened at Bethesda by the Reverend George Whitefield was said to have been the colony's most prominent institution of learning prior to 1775.

The schools founded by the S.P.G. had considerable influence on education in the South. One educational historian has claimed that these Society schools "furnished the nearest approach to a public school organization found in the South before the Revolution." Whatever the actuality of this contention, the S.P.G. charity schools were evidence of the fact that this Episcopal missionary society provided the foremost philanthropic movement in education during the colonial period.

Denominational schools established by non-Episcopal dissenters were found in all southern colonies. In Maryland, Roman Catholics established several schools, the earliest of which were the work of Robert Crouch, a planter and subsequently (1669) a Jesuit priest. Presbyterian schools were also established in Maryland, but the main areas where they proliferated were the Piedmont section of Virginia and the backwoods of the Carolinas. According to Carl Bridenbaugh, southern Quakers were slow in starting schools "although they had several in Virginia and North Carolina in 1775." German religious sects also conducted schools in Maryland and the Carolinas during the eighteenth century. In Georgia, the Moravians established the earliest school in the colony at Irene. Their later schools in Wachovia, North Carolina offered advanced education and admitted non-Moravians who would pay a fee. Most of these denominational schools, however, were restricted along religious lines, and with some exceptions, limited themselves to sectarian indoctrination and instruction in elementary subjects.

The "old field schools" existed in areas of the South where a substantial number of small planters or farmers worked their lands. Here these groups sometimes erected a schoolhouse on an old abandoned tobacco field—thus giving it the title "old field school." The communal effort behind these schools was noted by Virginia's historian Robert Beverley who wrote in 1705 that where endowed schools did not exist, "the people join and build schools for their children where they may learn on very easie terms." The schoolmaster was often the parish Episcopal priest or lay reader although indentured servants and planters' wives were used on occasion. The old field schools were supported by tuition charges on all students. Rarely did these schools offer instruction beyond the rudiments of learning, but for most of their students this was all that was desired.

Private venture schools existed throughout the South, but they were found in greatest number within the region's small number of sizable communities. Annapolis, Norfolk, Savannah, Baltimore, Richmond, and particularly Charleston had many self-appointed teachers who offered instruction. Although newspaper advertisements from this period highlighted private schoolmasters offering the more popular secondary-level subjects, there were a substantial number of teachers offering elementary-level instruction. The schoolmasters who offered such basic instruction included women, indentured servants, and even former English convicts. Qualified ministers or laymen established private schools in the smaller southern communities, but these teachers normally offered only the more advanced instruction.

As previously noted, the earliest form of tutorial education in the South was provided on an informal basis by individual parents. Later, the emergent planter gentry began to copy the English upper-class practice of employing a private tutor. In 1669 for example, John Carter ordered in his will that a servant be procured to teach his six-year-old son Robert "his books in English or Latin." Those who served as tutors came from varied backgrounds. Some planter children, including George Washington, received their first formal instruction from transported English convicts, but the vast majority were tutored by ministers, women, educated indentured servants, and college graduates. The tutor dispensed his elementary lessons within the planter's home or in a nearby building. His pupils were ordinarily the planter's children, although some planters allowed others on their self-contained estates the benefit of basic learning. The wealthier residents of the South's few urban centers, as well as the rural planters, also employed tutors.

The limitations of elementary education in the southern colonies emerge from this survey of the various formal educational institutions of the region. Despite the fact that several types of schools existed, the actual opportunities for obtaining schooling were regulated largely by social position. Upperclass children could expect the best training through private tutoring or private schooling. For those not among the privileged orders, elementary education could be a most uncertain matter despite the efforts of individual parents and religious groups. Even poor white and orphaned children, for whom legislatures sometimes took responsibility, were fortunate if they received the rudiments of learning.

Secondary Education

The opportunities for secondary education in the South were also class oriented and, as such, were more limited than elementary education. Under the region's aristocratic social order, only privileged children were generally deemed worthy for education beyond the rudiments. Southern legislatures, which had done little to promote elementary education, did even less to aid secondary schools. In addition, endowed, old field, charity, and denominational schools seldom went beyond basic education. The restrictive effects of this situation were very evident. As late as 1724 Virginia reported only two grammar schools, and in 1763 Governor Horatio Sharpe of Maryland wrote that his colony had "not even one good grammar school." Secondary education as a result devolved largely upon private venture schools and private tutoring.

There were relatively few exceptions to this secondary school pattern in the southern colonies. Only three endowed free schools (King William's School in Maryland, the Thomas Eaton School in Virginia, and the Free School in Charleston, South Carolina) apparently offered instruction above the elementary level. The Charleston Free School, the most notable of these institutions, opened with a curriculum that included the classics as well as such practical subjects as mathematics, surveying, navigation, and merchants accounts. Under the auspices of the S.P.G., the Reverend William Gay opened a school in Charleston that accentuated the classics although it was neither a charity school nor a free school. A few non-Episcopal denominational schools offered secondary training but they did not open until well into the eighteenth century. The Presbyterian academies in Maryland and North Carolina, and the Moravian schools at Wachovia are examples of this latter group. Probably the only other exception to such secondary educational patterns was the grammar school at Williamsburg, which trained boys for William and Mary College.

Most private venture schools offering secondary level studies were located in the South's few large communities. Charleston was the first of the towns to offer advanced instruction in private venture schools. By 1713, according to Professor Bridenbaugh, children who could afford it, "could receive as good an education at Charles Town as in any northern center." Those secondary private schools that did open in Charleston and in other significant southern towns were primarily boarding and nonboarding day schools, although evening schools operated in Baltimore, Charleston, and Savannah. All such schools, whether of the day or evening variety, charged fees that virtually excluded poor children.

The curriculum of these private venture schools was secularly oriented, with little or no attention given to religious studies. Among those secular subjects that were offered, the practical courses took precedence over classical studies. The subordination of Latin and Greek in these urban schools is illustrated by these advertisements for Charleston private schools:

At the house of Mrs. Delaweare on Broad Street is taught these sciences

Arithmetic	*Surveying*	*Astronomy*
Algebra	*Dialling*	*Gauging*
Geometry	*Navigation*	*Fortification*
Trigonometry		

* * *

Reading, Writing, Arithmetick vulgar and decimal, Geometry, Trigonometry plain and spherical, Mensuration of solid and superficial Bodies, Navigation, Surveying, Gaging, and many other useful Branches of the Mathematicks, Euclid's Elements, Italian, bookkeeping and Grammar, &c: explain'd and taught in the clearest manner by Archidbald Hamilton, *who may be heard of at Mr.* Coon's *Taylor in* Church-street. *N.B. He attends at any time and Place requir'd to teach, or to keep Books; and is willing upon a reasonable and speedy Encouragement to undertake a School in Town or Country for teaching all or any Part of what is above specified, otherwise to go off the country.*

In contrast to these urban private secondary schools, those located in the South's smaller towns tended to have a classically oriented curriculum. One such school accentuating Latin and Greek was opened by the Reverend James Mayre at Fredericksburg, Virginia in 1740. George Washington, James Madison, and James Monroe received all or part of their secondary training at this school. Thomas Jefferson gained his preparation for college at the Reverend James Maury's classical school in Albemarle County. Another Episcopal priest, the Reverend Jonathan Boucher, conducted boys boarding schools in Hanover and St. Mary's parishes. One of the Maryland schools that did accentuate a more utilitarian course of study was Somerset Academy. In an advertisement in the *Virginia Gazette* (February 23, 1769), the school costs were listed as £17 annually for a broad curriculum. "The scholars are taught the rudiments of English grammar, orthography or the art of spelling, and some portion of time is spent every week to perfect them in writing. They are instructed in the *Latin and Greek* languages and may be taught the various branches of the *arts and sciences*, such as geography, logick, navigation, surveying &c." A somewhat similar institution was opened near Newmarket, North Carolina by the Reverend David Caldwell, a Presbyterian minister.

All such private, secondary-level institutions had disadvantages, so the South's planter aristocrats relied more and more on tutorial education. For those plantation families who maintained a tutor qualified to teach both elementary and advanced subjects, the beneficial influences of home life could be maintained for a longer time. Many planters, therefore, went to considerable lengths to find a suitable tutor. In 1766, for example, Richard Corbin wrote as far as London seeking a qualified tutor, while six years later Landon Carter of Virginia advertised an offer of £50 plus maintenance to "any gentleman" who could teach his six grandsons. During the eighteenth century, tutors who were employed by the great planters were often treated as near social equals, and some even married into the planter's family.

The secondary instruction offered by tutors at their plantation schools was usually given on an individual basis and was classically oriented. Yet, in addition to Latin and Greek, some tutors taught mathematics and accounting to the planters' sons.

The eventual goal of such training was to fit these boys into their privileged position in southern society. More immediately, however, tutoring prepared planters' sons for colonial colleges, private-venture schools, the grammar school at William and Mary College, and sometimes for education abroad.

Southerners had begun the practice of sending their children abroad for education relatively early in their history. This fact is evident in the wills of several seventeenth-century Virginians that provided for the education of their children in Europe. Despite the considerable expense and the dangers involved in ocean travel, many affluent planters were eager to give their children the expected advantages of a European education. A few children were shipped off at a very young age, but most of those sent abroad were over the age of 10. Their family names—Byrd, Carroll, Fitzhugh, Randolph, Carter, Rutledge, Pinckney, and Laurens—were among the most prominent in the South and, of course, represented the comparative few who could bear the considerable costs.

English schools were the source of secondary education for most of these privileged southern youths. (An exception was the Jesuit school at St. Omer in Flanders, where the Roman Catholic Carrolls of Maryland sent their boys.) Some of the boys who went to the mother country attended prominent public schools such as Eton and Winchester, but lesser-known grammar and private schools were also frequented. Schools in this latter category even advertised in southern newspapers. In 1766, for example, the *Virginia Gazette* carried the notice of a broad curriculum offered at the Reverend B. Booth's academy near Liverpool, and three years later it carried a similar advertisement for an "Academy" in Leeds, Yorkshire.

By this time, however, the practice of sending children abroad for education was already losing its former popularity. In 1765, Peter Timothy of South Carolina complained that the colony was drained of £2000 annually, while in 1770 Virginia's Landon Carter noted, "I believe everybody begins to laugh at English education; the general importers of it nowadays bring back only a stiff priggishness with as little good manners as possible."

Higher Education

There were several unsuccessful attempts to establish colleges in the colonial South. In Maryland, a plan for the establishment of a college was brought before the legislature without result. Similar proposals in 1732, 1754, 1761, and 1773 also failed. In 1723 a scheme for establishing an Episcopal college in South Carolina was bypassed in the Assembly. More vigorous attempts to found a college in or near Charleston were made in 1764 and 1770, but the pre-Revolutionary tensions prevented their success. In January 1771 the North Carolina legislature actually chartered a higher level institution called "Queen's College" located in Charlotte. The charter, however, was promptly disallowed by the King and his council. In Georgia, a plan for a college was submitted by the Reverend George Whitefield, but it also was rejected in England.

Virginia also experienced some unsuccessful attempts to found colleges, but eventually became the only southern colony to have an institution of higher education. The first attempt began in 1619 when the Virginia Company reserved 10,000 acres and collected subscriptions for a "university to be at Henrico" with a missionary branch for Indian education. Despite the Company's endeavors, however, nothing resulted from this project. Later, in 1661, the Virginia General Assembly passed an act authorizing a "colledge and free school," and the King was afterward petitioned for letters of patent to raise funds. Although several contributions, both in money and tobacco, were given, this effort also failed. Substantial subscriptions for a college were made in 1688-1689 by certain English merchants, but again without immediate results. Finally, in 1691, the Reverend James Blair, Episcopal Commissary for Virginia, was sent by the colony's Assembly to England to secure a college charter from skeptical English officials. To one of his arguments that a college would train ministers to save Virginian souls, the British Lord Treasurer is said to have replied, "Souls! Damn your souls! Make tobacco!" Yet, Blair's efforts were finally successful, and the royal charter of 1693 marked the foundation of the College of William and Mary.

The College did not operate to the full extent envisaged in its charter until several years after its founding. Despite the energetic efforts of its first president, the Reverend Mr. Blair, the college was able to open only its grammar school by the close of the seventeenth century. The first building on its Middle Plantation (Williamsburg) site was not completed until 1700, while its faculty at this time numbered only two. Some College-level instruction finally began about 1712, but it was not until 1729 that the full six professorships called for in the charter were filled and serious teaching began. Afterward, William and Mary became a more highly regarded institution and included among its noted pre-Revolutionary students Thomas Jefferson, John Marshall, and James Monroe.

Many educational aspects of William and Mary College were similar to those of Harvard and Yale. Like its New England counterparts, William and Mary was a sectarian institution which had a primary purpose of supplying churches with an orthodox ministry. Its founder proposed that the new college was to see "that the Church of Virginia [Episcopal] may be furnished with a seminary of ministers of the Gospel . . . ." In this respect all three early colonial colleges called for orthodoxy among their faculty, required a classical grounding in Latin and Greek for admission, and instituted strict rules for moral and religious conduct by its students. Yet, despite this common stress on religion, Harvard, Yale, and William and Mary also prepared prospective lawyers and physicians as well as ministers for colonial service. Recognizing this important professional role of such institutions, the colonial legislatures that helped found these colleges also granted certain privileges to their faculties and gave needed financial assistance to the colleges themselves. In the case of William and Mary, the Virginia Assembly made substantial land and money grants to the college and also gave it income from duties on skins, furs, and exported tobacco. Also, following an English parliamentary practice, the college was allowed to send a representative to Virginia's legislative assembly.

The administration of William and Mary contained a few features that differed from other colonial colleges. Under its original charter of 1693 the management of college affairs was left to dual governing bodies, one being the "Faculty," and the other a board of nonresident "Visitors." The Faculty unit consisted of the college president and the masters (professors), while the Visitors were a self-perpetuating body of fourteen laymen and four clerics who were originally selected by the Virginia legislature. Initially, the Faculty was expected to manage business affairs and the Visitors were to appoint faculty members and make the college rules or statutes. Eventually, faculty representatives at William and Mary were able to achieve a greater degree of autonomy than at other colonial colleges, largely through a limited right of appeal to England. By the outbreak of the American Revolution, however, the Board of Visitors still held the principal control over the college.

During the eighteenth century, the curriculum at William and Mary experienced significant changes. Originally, the course of study was geared to meet the needs of the college's three departments: the grammar school, the school of philosophy, and the school of sacred theology. As such, the early curriculum was classically oriented and was quite similar to that of Harvard College. By the early 1700's, however, President Blair began to break with traditional studies. In 1716 Mr. William Levingstone was allowed to teach dancing to the students, and the following year, the Reverend Hugh Jones was appointed to the college's chair of mathematics. When the college reached its full complement of six professors in 1729, it broadened its curriculum even further. New courses in mathematics, science, law, and philosophy were introduced, and in 1779 the William and Mary curriculum was reorganized into probably the most advanced in the United States.

Despite its more progressive curriculum and increased popularity, the College of William and Mary was subjected to serious criticism during the decades immediately preceding the American Revolution. One Virginia planter declared that he had "known the Professors to play at night at cards in publick houses in the city and . . . . often seen them drunk in the street." Another planter, William Randolph, even stipulated in his will that under no circumstances should his son be sent to the college. A few privileged southern boys such as William Hooper (Harvard, 1760) and James Madison (Princeton, 1771) were educated in northern colleges, but the overwhelming majority of those not receiving higher education at William and Mary were sent to England for study.

Wealthy southern families showed considerable attachment to English higher education during most of the colonial period. Generally these planter aristocrats ignored those who emphasized the values of a William and Mary education. Instead, they strove to give their sons the broadened educational and social advantages available in Great Britain. Many southern boys sent abroad went solely for higher education, but there were several who had been sent to England for their grammar-school training and remained for an advanced education. For their collegiate training they studied at Oxford, Cambridge, or the University of Edinburgh. For professional training in law, southern students enrolled at the Inns of Court and Lincoln's Fields. Edinburgh was the center of medical training. Ellwood Cubberley has pointed out that most of the 63 Americans who took degrees there between 1760 and 1775 were from the South. Pre-Revolutionary tensions, as previously noted, did restrict such overseas study though the effects appear greater on the secondary rather than the higher educational level.

Teachers and Textbooks

Individuals who entered the teaching profession in the southern colonies came from varied backgrounds. Some were young college graduates who had accepted temporary positions as tutors on plantations while awaiting a more permanent career. Others were also college graduates who had opened their own private schools, either on a permanent basis or while awaiting a ministerial call. Even some established ministers undertook teaching to supplement their limited income. Virginia's church wardens and parish readers or clerks sometimes acted as teachers in local schools although they were not required to do so. For southern Episcopal missionaries, however, education was a primary responsibility. Indentured servants and transported convicts often accepted teaching as a less arduous means of obtaining their freedom. Lastly, there were numerous self-appointed, unqualified teachers; often adventurers or misfits who had failed in other occupations turned to teaching as a final resort. Such individuals often hindered the South's already limited educational opportunities even more.

Although the South failed to produce educational equals to New England's Ezekiel Cheever and Elijah Corlett, the region did have its noteworthy teachers. One such individual was Philip Fithian, a Princeton graduate who served as a tutor on the Virginia plantation of Robert Carter. Fithian wrote an extremely fascinating and often-quoted diary of his experiences, in which he described not only the nature of tutorial education but also life on a colonial plantation. Another graduate, the Reverend David Caldwell, received notoriety from his "Log College" in North Carolina. Students came from all over the South to attend this Presbyterian school that reportedly enjoyed the greatest reputation in the region for its type of education.

In the realm of higher education, two prominent William and Mary teachers were William Small, a professor of science, and Hugh Jones, the college's first professor of mathematics and natural philosophy. Jones was also known for his *An Accidence to the English Tongue* (London, 1724), the first English grammar written in America. Nevertheless, the college's most prestigious member during this period was undoubtedly James Blair, its founder and president from 1693 to 1743.

In the South, as in New England, there were occasional attempts to certify or license schoolmasters. During 1684, for example, the governor of Virginia ordered that all teachers must come to Jamestown to present testimonials as to their competency from leading citizens of their parishes. Fifteen years later county clerks were required to investigate all the schools in their jurisdiction together with statements on whether or not the teachers had licenses from the governor or the Bishop of London. Other southern colonies enacted similar requirements, and in 1714 the region fell under the provisions of England's Schism Act that stated that no one was allowed to offer any form of instruction without the Bishop of London's permission. Although England subsequently repealed the act, it continued to be used sporadically in the South. Sometimes Episcopal church membership was required for certain school positions as were oaths of allegiance for all schoolmasters in a particular colony. However, the continual teacher shortage in all colonies worked against any consistent policy of licensing every teacher or carefully examining their capabilities. Maryland Governor John Hart's statement of 1714 was quite relevant to this situation: "Good schoolmasters are very much wanting; What we have are very insufficient and of their being qualified by the Bishop of London or governor's license, it has been entirely neglected."

The textbooks used in southern schools were similar to those in New England. Children in both regions generally learned their ABC's, reading, writing, and basic arithmetic from hornbooks, "Battledoors," primers, psalters, and the Scriptures. At the secondary level of education both New England and southern boys were introduced to the classics through *Accidences*,

Nomenclators, and vocabularies. Thomas Dilworth's *A New Guide to the English Tongue* was somewhat less prominent in southern schools than in New England due to the use in the South of Hugh Jones' English grammar. Schools in both colonial regions also made considerable use of James Hodder, Edward Cocker, or Thomas Dilworth's arithmetics during the eighteenth century. Textbooks in higher education, except for those of a strictly sectarian nature, were about the same at Episcopal William and Mary as at Congregational Harvard and Yale.

Girls' Education

Southern girls, like New England girls, were subject to restrictive educational attitudes and practices. In the South, the limitations were probably even more pronounced since Anglicans did not share the Puritan's religious belief that both sexes must be imbued with a knowledge and understanding of the Scriptures. Both colonial regions, however, shared the same conception that the capacities of girls could never equal those of boys. Therefore, no need was felt to saturate a young girl's mind with Greek and Latin inasmuch as she would not be allowed to enter the realm of higher education. Aside from a knowledge of cooking and sewing, instruction in reading, writing, and basic arithmetic formed the bounds of educational aspirations for most southern girls.

Distinctions between the sexes were made in informal educational practices within the South. Boys and girls were both subject to apprenticeship legislation in the southern colonies, but they did not always receive the same nonvocational instructional benefits from their masters. It was already noted, for example, that Virginia, which in 1705 and 1727 had placed requirements on the masters of male apprentices to instruct them in reading and writing, did not enact corresponding requirements for girls until 1751 for reading and 1769 for writing. Similar discrimination occurred in the apprenticeship patterns of other southern colonies. Among children who received instruction within the household, the boys were usually given much more attention than the girls. As one southern colonial historian has indicated, girls were taught at home mainly to do those things that would make them a good wife and house-keeper.

Those southern women who had received elementary in-struction usually obtained it in one of the region's formal agencies for schooling. S.P.G. charity schools and dame schools were generally open to girls as well as boys. Some girls also studied in the old field, private venture, and endowed free schools of southern parishes. Moravians, Presbyterians, and Quakers usually opened their elementary level schools on a co-educational basis in backwoods areas. In the South's few urban centers many private elementary level schools were opened, some on a coeducational basis. Finally, there were the numer-ous plantation schools where tutors were expected to devote some of their attention to instructing the owner's daughters.

Secondary educational opportunities for girls were more re-stricted. Endowed free schools and most private schools that offered advanced instruction were not open to girls. Neverthe-less, there were some private schools in the South's few towns that catered to females and advertised such relatively advanced level subjects as music, dancing, French, embroidery, and watercoloring. Affluent girls from the countryside often boarded in towns in order to receive instruction at such so-called "finishing schools." Daughters of the gentry who remained on a plantation had less opportunity for this type of schooling. Aside from dancing instruction and possibly reading some of the books from the plantation house library, they seldom had the opportunity for any secondary education.

Secondary training in private town schools marked the limits of female education in the colonial South. These private second-ary level schools were normally segregated according to sex, although Charleston's "British Academy on the Green," founded in 1769 did mark a new beginning for coeducational studies. Yet, the overall effect of this educational innovation was not very great. The beginning of the American Revolution still found southern girls excluded from any preparation for an advanced liberal education. And it was rather natural, therefore, that the stepfather of one prominent Virginia girl found it merely amusing when she "thought it hard they would not teach me Greek and Latin because I was a girl—they laughed and said women ought not to know these things."

Indian and Negro Education

The patterns of education previously described applied to the children of white southerners. Instructional opportunities for the region's Indian and Negro inhabitants composed a largely separate category.

Most of the South's first settlers, like the ones in New England, did not regard the Indian inhabitants with bitter hostility. Instead, the Virginia Company merchants of London were desirous of maintaining the friendship of the natives, primarily for economic motives. It was hoped that an amicable and docile Indian population might serve as a source of foodstuffs and labor for the compact fort-factory settlements that merchants envisaged for Virginia. Educating the natives to the ways of Englishmen, therefore, became part of the efforts of the Virginia Company and, afterward, the royal government.

Most seventeenth-century attempts to educate the South's Indian population proved unsuccessful, however. The first of these efforts began in 1619 with the Virginia Company's endeavors to establish an Indian school as part of the proposed college at Henrico. "A convenient number of Indian boys" were to be sent to this school annually for instruction in reading and the principles of the Christian religion, and after the age of 14 they were to be taught some handicraft. The scheme eventually collapsed in the wake of a sudden Indian uprising in 1622 that took the lives of 347 Virginians. A subsequent serious uprising in 1644 further deteriorated Indian-white relations and left most Virginians with little enthusiasm for educating the natives. Anglican clergymen such as the Reverend Peter Heylyn criticized the absence of missionary zeal, but little was done about educating the South's Indians until almost the close of the century. The proposed school at William and Mary for teaching Indian boys the "three R's" and religion was not functioning until the eighteenth century, and even then Indian youths did not flock to attend it.

Somewhat more substantial efforts toward educating the Indians were made during the eighteenth century. The chief agency in the South for this charitable work was the Society for the Propagation of the Gospel in Foreign Parts. This Episcopal missionary society had as one of its main purposes "bringing heathen to the knowledge of the truth." Its missionaries and teachers were instructed to be prepared for teaching Indian and Negro children as well as white children. Active in all southern colonies but Virginia, the Society's workers instructed thousands of Indians in religion and sometimes reading and writing. Reports to the Society in London listed their educational achievements as well as the obstacles that these missionaries and workers encountered. Among such obstacles were disease, primitive living conditions, and opposition from settlers, including fellow Anglicans. Although the Moravians and Presbyterians also performed missionary work and instructed southern Indians, their philanthropic efforts did not match those of the S.P.G. during this period.

It was already noted that the first Negroes arrived in Virginia in 1619, and that many of the small number who came before the middle of the century were evidently treated much like white servants and released after a term of service. These circumstances, however, did not last. During the latter half of the seventeenth century, southern colonies used the factor of color to fix upon the growing numbers of blacks the status of chattel slavery. The South, with its emergent plantation system, became the center of Negro population for the continental colonies. Virginia, which according to Oscar Handlin had only

250 Negroes in 1640, had 16,400 in 1700 and 187,000 out of a population of 447,000 in 1770. South Carolina in 1770 had three black residents for every two whites. Maryland, Georgia, and North Carolina also had many Negro inhabitants—most of them slaves. Altogether there were over 420,000 Negroes in the South by the American Revolution, about 25 times more than those living in New England.

Slavery was a cruel, debasing institution in which southern society, almost constantly in fear of insurrection, applied extremely harsh restrictions upon their chattels. Slaves were often beaten at will by their masters, mistresses, and overseers without having recourse to civil authorities. In other cases they were chained, branded, or mutilated despite the cash value they had to their owners. Slaves accused of crimes were given none of the usual protections of English common law, and their rights were ignored in the interest of meting out summary justice. They could be arrested, tried, and convicted solely on the evidence of a single witness, and after 1692 Virginia denied them the right of trial by jury. Generally, the killing of a Negro was not a punishable offense, but southern slaves found guilty of murdering their masters were hung, beheaded, and drawn and quartered.

In line with such repressive treatment, most southern whites frowned on the idea of educating slaves. Slavery required submissiveness, obedience, and servility—qualities that were not enhanced by education. Teaching a slave or a freed Negro to read or write, or even instructing him in the principles of Christianity was often regarded as a threat to the white community. Black children, therefore, were excluded from the southern legislation that obligated masters to instruct their apprentices in reading and writing. In addition, legislation such as the following South Carolina statute of 1740 specifically prohibited certain instruction:

And whereas, *the having of slaves taught to write, or suffering them to be employed in writing, may be attended with great in-*

convenience; Be it therefore enacted *by the authority aforesaid, That all and every person or persons whatsoever, who shall hereafter teach, or cause any slave or slaves to be taught, to write, or shall employ any slave as a scribe in any manner of writing whatsoever, hereafter taught to write, every such person or persons, shall, for every offense, forfeit the sum of one hundred pounds current money.*

Despite these obstacles efforts were occasionally made in southern colonies to offer some form of instruction to Negroes. In Virginia, for example, the Reverend James Blair tried unsuccessfully to gain legislative approval for a plan whereby Indian, Negro, and Mulatto children would be catechized and given religious instruction by the local parish priest. One such Episcopal priest, the Reverend Thomas Bacon, did establish a short-lived charity school in St. Peter's Parish in 1750 that offered elementary education to orphans, poor children, and Negroes. Other limited educational opportunities apparently existed on an informal basis from time to time. One colonial historian has cited a document from pre-Revolutionary Virginia stating that the planter William Hunter "paid Ann wages for teaching at Negro Schools." As in the realm of Indian education, however, the most notable achievements in offering religious and secular instruction were made by the S.P.G. Their generally diligent efforts in the face of considerable difficulties gave many of the degraded black men, women, and children at least a modicum of learning.

Charleston experienced the most conspicuous educational undertakings of all southern communities. In 1740 a certain Mr. Boulson, the operator of a "Dancing School, Ball, Assembly Concert Room Etc.," converted his institution into a school for Negroes after he had experienced a religious conversion. According to Carl Bridenbaugh, Boulson soon had 53 students, and although he was briefly brought to court for teaching blacks to read, he was subsequently allowed to resume his work. In 1743 the S.P.G. founded a school in the town for

"Homeborn" black children under 10 years of age to be taught by Negro instructors. The school was discontinued in 1764 for lack of Negro teachers, but during its existence this school taught an annual average of 60 Negro children to read the Scriptures. Yet, these minor educational efforts in Charleston were of little overall benefit to the South's suffering black populace. Even at the time of the Declaration of Independence most southerners still found it inconceivable that Negroes should share in the natural rights of mankind.

* * * * *

Southern educational achievements were quite limited during the colonial period. The region's scattered pattern of settlement, the indifferent attitude of resident Episcopal clergymen, and the general wish to emulate England's prevailing learning practices all combined to restrict the South's educational progress during the seventeenth century. One colonial historian has estimated that by 1700 only 55 percent of the men and 25 percent of the women in Virginia could write their names. During the eighteenth century new apprenticeship legislation, plus the work of the S.P.G. and other religious denominations, improved the South's educational picture somewhat. Even William and Mary, the only southern colonial college, made significant progress in higher learning after 1700. Basically, however, the amount of learning most southerners received was still regulated by their position within the region's generally aristocratic social structure. By 1776, therefore, the South's illiteracy level remained well above New England's, with no satisfactory system of schooling in sight.

education in the middle colonies, 1607-1776

That area of colonial America that was known as the "Middle Colonies" lay between the South and New England. The four colonies founded in this section—New York, New Jersey, Pennsylvania, and Delaware—often contained an admixture of the patterns found in the regions to their immediate north and south. This combination was evident in particular features such as local governmental practices, economic occupations, extent of individual land holdings, and the intellectual pursuits of many of the settlers. The middle-ground appearance remained a prominent characteristic of the region throughout the colonial period. In fact, it persisted well into the nineteenth century.

Besides the admixture of influences from its regional neighbors, life in the Middle Colonies was also marked by the factor of diversity. Not only did the inhabitants of this colonial section display wide dissimilarities in their Old World background, but they also succeeded in establishing much of their varied European heritages in their New World settlements. Differences in language, traditions, religious faiths, and political theories were far more distinct in the Middle Colonies than in the South or New England. These differences also produced effects on the region itself. Although the divergent cultures

151

of the Middle Colonies led to a general pattern of religious toleration and disestablishment, this same diversity also thwarted any unified efforts toward erecting common social institutions. This lack of joint societal resolve was particularly evident in the field of education.

Because education in the Middle Colonies generally lacked this common social unity, many educational historians have found it convenient to survey the region on the basis of individual colonies. This method was followed by early historians of American education as well as by several contemporary scholars. In a section of such contrasting cultures and beliefs, this approach has definite advantages. While some similar educational features did carry over from one colony to another, the region, for the most part, contained far more diversified learning practices than the other colonial sections. This concluding chapter therefore, will examine the educational structure of the Middle Colonies within the context of each colony's learning practices.

The New Netherlands Colony

The voyage of Henry Hudson to America in 1609 under the sponsorship of the Dutch East India Company marked the origin of New Netherlands. Active colonization of Hudson's territorial claims did not commence until the 1620s, however, when a new agency, the Dutch West India Company, was granted a trade monopoly over all Dutch lands in the Western Hemisphere. The main company settlements in continental North America existed along the Hudson river from New Amsterdam to Fort Orange (Albany), though their trading posts were established from Delaware Bay to New England. Because of its location and commercial successes, New Netherlands inevitably conflicted with its English neighbors. A series of Anglo-Dutch Wars gave England the opportunity to seize the weaker New Netherlands holdings in 1664. Then, 10 years later, the colony was formally ceded to England by the Treaty of Westminster.

During its existence, New Netherlands had attracted a relatively small but diverse group of settlers. The entire population by 1665 was below 10,000, but these inhabitants represented quite varied national backgrounds. In addition to Dutchmen, the settlers included Englishmen, Scotch-Irish, Frenchmen, Swedes, Finns, and Italians. (One French missionary reported in 1643 that 18 different languages were spoken in New Amsterdam alone.) This heterogeneity of nationalities gave New Netherlands a distinctly international character. At the same time, however, it served to thwart any possibilities for social unity.

The colony's mixed population also affected the nature of its governmental and religious institutions. In the former case, the Dutch West India Company had delegated judicial, legislative and administrative authority over the colony to a director-general and a small advisory council. No provisions were made for a system of representative authority—a fact that often caused discontent and remonstrances among the non-Dutch inhabitants.

In addition to unrest over this arbitrary and centralized control, many of the resident minority groups became discontented over religious affairs. The Dutch Reformed Church was considered the colony's established faith, but several other Protestant sects as well as a few Jews and Roman Catholics also practiced their beliefs in New Netherlands. These dissenters—most whom had been attracted by the company's promises of spiritual freedom—were sensitive to the slightest religious restriction or attempts to enhance the powers of the official church. Consequently, harassment of dissenter sects by director-generals such as Peter Stuyvesant served only to deepen the colony's extensive religious divisions and enmities.

New Netherland's chief purpose was commercial, but the Dutch West India Company was unable to make its territory an economic success. Although several traders settled in the colony, the company had difficulty attracting farmers to the region. An attempt to solve the problem of agricultural production occurred when large tracts of land were offered to "patroons," or landlords, who were required to bring with them at least 50 tenants. The patroons were even granted semi-feudal powers over their estates and tenants, although, in the American environment, the system proved unworkable. Despite the existence of some manageable small farms and the substantial overseas commerce centered in New Amsterdam, New Netherlands failed to enrich its Dutch stockholders. Hence, its eventual surrender and cession to England caused little furor in Holland.

Education in New Netherlands

Despite the fact that education in New Netherlands was considered a mutual concern of church and state, both institutions did comparatively little to effectively meet this responsibility. There were several reasons for such general inaction. The diversity of national stocks and religious creeds made it difficult for the Dutch West India Company to formulate a comprehensive educational policy. The scattered pattern of settlement within the colony was another deterrent. An absence of representative government at the colony and local levels was another factor impeding educational development. Finally, the dominant materialistic motivations of the Company directors restricted the incentive of colony officials to establish and maintain a compulsory system of schooling.

Education, however, was not completely ignored. In New Netherlands, as in New England and the South, the family and the apprenticeship system served as the two principal means for informal education. Regardless of their national origins, the colony's various family groups gave their offspring their first moral, ethical, and sectarian instruction. Although the extent of such training usually differed according to each family's particular circumstance, many children in New Netherlands attained literacy through informal home instruction.

Apprenticeship practices brought over from Holland offered

many children an opportunity for a vocational education and sometimes training in reading and writing. New Netherlands enacted no apprenticeship legislation comparable to Massachusetts Bay, but apprenticeship contracts, which included requirements for basic educational instruction, were considered legally binding by Dutch officials. To satisfy these obligations many of the colony's masters instructed their apprentices along with their own children in reading and writing.

On the formal level of instruction, authorities in Dutch America did concern themselves about education. The close ties between learning and the established faith that existed in Holland were recreated in New Netherlands. In both the colony and the mother country the state was expected to promote the aims of the official church. Since one of the chief purposes of the Dutch Reform Church was to imbue their children in orthodox Calvinist teachings, it therefore became a duty of secular authorities to facilitate the founding of schools.

In Holland the responsibility for the maintenance of education was delegated to the magistrates, while the school's administrative affairs were generally handled by local religious synods. In New Netherlands, however, this parochial system of learning was modified. There the obligation for school maintenance rested with the West India Company while operational functions were conducted by the Classis of Amsterdam. The Company was accordingly expected to locate a school site, furnish school equipment, make school repairs, and pay most of the schoolmaster's salary. The Classis of Amsterdam, consisting of representatives from Amsterdam's churches, examined, licensed, and often selected the schoolmasters dispatched to the New World. It also played an indirect role in supervising the schoolmasters sent there. Yet despite this division of authority, both the Classis and the Company were 3000 miles from New Netherlands. Unlike Holland therefore, direct supervision over the establishment and operation of the colony's schools was considerably weakened.

Although the Classis of Amsterdam and the West India Company had acknowledged the problem of education in New Netherlands during the 1620s, no successful achievements were made until the following decade. It was then that the first official school was founded in New Amsterdam. While several educational historians have given the date of establishment as 1633, William H. Kilpatrick, a noted scholar on New Netherlands education noted that "it was improbable that there was any official schoolmaster licensed prior to August 4, 1637, and that there was any official school before 1638." The Dutch schoolmaster who was licensed by the Classis in 1637 was Adam Roelantsen, a former settler in the colony. After receiving his certification in Holland, Roelantsen departed for New Amsterdam where he apparently opened his school during the spring of 1638.

Roelantsen served as town schoolmaster for about four years. During this period he was far less than a symbol of respect in the community. He was consistently involved in lawsuits, and upon several occasions was accused of disorderly and immoral conduct and slander. Eventually, he was ordered to be publicly whipped for one of his numerous offenses, whereupon he abandoned his position. Most of Roelantsen's successors as town schoolmaster also proved unsatisfactory. One reason for this general inability to attract qualified schoolmasters was the meager salaries offered, and another reason was the extra duties required of the instructor. Often Roelantsen and his successors found themselves obligated to serve as church sextant, process server, and grave digger in addition to their instructional tasks. This situation naturally demeaned the professional status of the community's schoolmasters.

The New Amsterdam school where these masters taught was operated on an elementary level. It offered instruction in reading, writing, religion and, occasionally, basic arithmetic. Girls as well as boys were admitted to the school at about age seven, though the sexes were separated within the classroom. Since dame schools rarely existed in the colony, children usually entered the school unprepared except for whatever instruction they received at home. The school was open to all the community's children, but since its religious instruction was based upon the teachings of the established Reformed Church, attendance by children of dissenters was undoubtedly rare.

Provisions for the school's formal operation were made through the joint efforts of the West India Company and civil and religious officials in America. School books, paper, slates, and other supplies were furnished by the Company. New Amsterdam's magistrates provided the school site, which was usually in the schoolmaster's home or a public house in the community. Supervision over school instruction was provided by local civil and religious officials. The schoolmaster was permitted to collect fees as part of his salary from all his students except those who were "poor and needy." The greater part of the teacher's salary, however, was paid by the director-general from local taxes levied by the town. These taxes or fees were levied only on specific items, such as liquor licenses, and were not assessed on the general population. Because the tax was not general and because of the sectarian nature of the curriculum, it is erroneous to regard New Amsterdam's school as a "public" institution in a modern sense.

In addition to New Amsterdam, most other chartered settlements in New Netherlands founded elementary-level schools. Among these communities were Midwoud (Flatbush), Flatlands, Bushwick, Beverwyck (Albany), Wiltwyck (Kingston), Bergen (Newark), Breacklen (Brooklyn) and New Haerlem. In the case of Beverwyck, the patroons assumed the company's role in establishing the local school. Nevertheless, these schools were not opened until the latter years of Dutch control, and they generally operated on an irregular basis. This absence of a regularly functioning school system was a serious matter to many of the colony's Dutch inhabitants. In the Great Remonstrance of 1649 many of them lamented the decayed state of education throughout New Netherlands. These residents then recommended to Holland's legislature that "there should be a public school provided in New Amsterdam with at least two good masters so that first of all in so wild a country where there are so many loose people, the youth may be well taught and brought up not only in reading and writing, but also in the knowledge and fear of the Lord." The Dutch government, however, continued to do practically nothing to aid the colony's elementary level schools.

As for education beyond the elementary level, little was done until the final years of the Dutch rule. A Latin school was reportedly started but soon abandoned in a New Amsterdam "city tavern" during 1652. Six years later, several of the town's prominent residents petitioned the company's directors for a Latin master. The directors sent Dr. Alexander Carolus Curtius to New Amsterdam in early 1659. Curtius served as schoolmaster from July, 1659 to July 1661, but was dismissed after he proved unpopular with the parents and a poor student disciplinarian. His position remained unfilled until 1662 when Aegidius Luyck became the new Latin instructor. Luyck, once a tutor to Director-General Stuyvesant's children proved much more respected than Dr. Curtius and remained as schoolmaster until shortly after New Amsterdam's capture by the English.

There were additional schools or means of instruction in New Netherlands. Children of the non-Dutch settlers who received an education outside their homes were often taught by their own clergymen. Several private teachers such as Jacques Cortelyou, Jan Juriaens Becker, and Johannes Van Gelden were licensed and offered their instructional abilities. New Netherlands even established an evening school in 1661 where, after work, boys and adults might learn reading and writing or vocational studies. Nevertheless, for most of the colony's children only a meager education was available.

In the final analysis, New Netherland's educational structure was determined by its Dutch overseers. These rulers had reproduced as much of Holland's parochial school system as American conditions permitted. The result was a mixture of direct and indirect secular and religious regulation over the schools that were successfully established within the colony. Although these Dutch schools did not represent the beginnings of modern public education as some educational historians have argued, they nonetheless represented the sincere effort of New England's leaders to provide a basic education for their children. This effort in itself was probably the colony's most important educational legacy.

New Netherlands Becomes New York

The conquest of New Netherlands in 1664 by its English neighbors marked the beginnings of profound changes in the colony's administration. Along with other territories these lands in Dutch America were granted as a proprietorship by King Charles II to his brother James, Duke of York. The Duke received almost unlimited power over his American estates. Then following the seizure of New Netherlands by one of his deputies, the province and its chief settlement were renamed in his honor. The Duke, however, chose not to exert direct control over the former Dutch province. Instead, he appointed a governor and a council who were expected to rule New York for the proprietor. The Duke of York's government proved comparatively liberal and benevolent despite its aristocratic composition. During the two decades following New Netherland's capture, the Duke's administrators placated the conquered Dutch inhabitants, established English law, promoted trade and commerce, and even permitted the meeting of a representative assembly.

Additional governmental changes for New York commenced in 1685. In that year the Duke of York ascended the English throne as James II and his proprietary province then became a royal colony. Three years later King James was deposed by the Glorious Revolution, but the colony continued to retain its royal status. The governor and his council were appointed by the Crown although by the beginning of the eighteenth century, New York also had a legislature with an elected lower house. Despite its early tenuous status, this lower house gradually emerged as an influential governmental body. Its membership struggled repeatedly to enhance local interests, and their successes by the end of the colonial period had significantly reduced royal authority within New York.

At the same time, other developments were occurring in New York. One such development was its extensive population growth. In 1665 the colony had only about 9,000 inhabitants while New York City contained roughly 1500 residents. By the outbreak of the American Revolution the colony's settlers numbered over 175,000 and New York City's population was approximately 23,000. These later settlers continued to represent a wide variety of national origins; in fact many immigrants from areas formerly unrepresented in the region arrived after the fall of New Netherlands. Those peoples who had immigrated following the English capture settled not only in New York City and along the Hudson River, but also helped found new communities in the more-remote Mohawk Valley.

Economic changes were also taking place. Agricultural production flourished partly on the large estates granted by the new English rulers, but even more on the colony's proliferating small farms. By the middle of the eighteenth century the remarkable rise in the production of foodstuffs was reflected in the fact that New York was exporting 80,000 barrels of flour annually. The fur trade, which had been fostered initially by the Dutch, was further broadened under English control. Lumbering was stimulated in the eighteenth century by the erection of numerous sawmills, the production of naval stores, and the construction of ships. The distilling industry expanded after the fall of New Netherlands, and several iron mills were established. All of these industries served as incentives to increased commercial expansion, with the port of New York steadily developing into another colonial center for an extensive overseas trade.

New societal alignments paralleled New York's broadened economic structure. A landed gentry emerged from the extensive estates granted under English control. These landed proprietors, who often operated their "manors" much like Southern plantations, shared the top of the colony's social structure with wealthy New York City merchants engaged in this community's lucrative commercial trade. A great many of New York's rural gentry were themselves successful merchants as well as planters. Below this narrow, upper level of society was a middle-class grouping of artisans, small farmers, petty tradesmen, and others of moderate means. Indentured servants and unskilled laborers composed the next social class grouping. At the base of the social structure were the Indians and Negroes. Negro slave labor was actually introduced by the Dutch, but it expanded under English control to such a point that by 1700 New York had more black slaves than any other northern colony.

Religious patterns were partially altered following the English annexation of New Netherlands. The Dutch Reformed Church was no longer the official church, but Anglicanism became the established faith only in New York's four lower counties. After the beginning of the eighteenth century, schoolmasters and missionaries of the Society for the Propagation of the Gospel were particularly active in spreading their religious tenets throughout the colony. Even so, the number of Anglican communicants remained relatively small during much of the century preceding the American Revolution. The principal feature of New York's religious composition was its sectarian diversity, a characteristic that continued beyond the era of Dutch control. Churches of numerous denominations thrived within this varied theological environment. However, while this constant religious diversity did influence the large measure of toleration that developed under English rule, it simultaneously perpetuated the colony's parochial spirit that thwarted the development of a uniform educational system.

Despite these elements of diversity and change, intellectual progress in New York was limited. The writings of the European Enlightenment were read in the colony, but most of the settler's attitudes remained dominated by commercialism. Bostonians looked on New Yorkers as "unintellectual and material," while many Southerners thought them "pushing, unrefined, and in general somewhat crude." To a considerable extent the colony's educational structure reflected the spirit of these comments.

Education in the Colony of New York

The English seizure of New Netherlands inevitably affected the educational patterns of New Amsterdam and its other Dutch settlements. Until 1674, all Dutch schools were permitted to operate virtually unchanged and the government of New York City even acknowledged its responsibility for the school rent and partial payment of the schoolmaster's salary. Afterwards, however, the city instituted changes regarding school support. The community's Dutch school was deprived of any funds from the civil purse, and the complete responsibility for control and support of this elementary level institution was left entirely to the Reformed Church. As a result, the school became a parochial institution with the civil officials merely licensing its appointed masters. It was maintained as the school of the Reformed Dutch Church of New York City and, as the Collegiate School, it has had a continuous existence from the colonial period to the present. A similar Dutch parochial institution was founded in New York City in 1743, but it lasted only 14 years.

In Dutch communities outside New York City, educational changes were less marked. Schools were established or continued to operate according to Dutch customs. Both civil and religious officials worked jointly in supervising the settlement's educational arrangements and they generally retained the right to approve the local schoolmaster. These local officials also maintained the practice of obligating the schoolmaster to perform additional after-school civil and religious duties. In those communities with a somewhat mixed population, the existing instruction was usually offered in both Dutch and English. In settlements that were entirely Dutch, the teaching was usually given in the Dutch tongue, at least throughout the remainder of the seventeenth century. Like the Reformed Church school in New York City, the aim of these local Dutch schools was to perpetuate Old World identities within their new environment.

Gradually, however, the Dutch schools succumbed to English influences or, as in the case of the New Harlem school, they were abandoned. With the passage of time following Holland's surrender of the colony, these institutions found it more difficult to resist the pressures toward assimilation. The impracticality of a purely Dutch education became increasingly apparent as English influences predominated over New York's cultural and commercial environment. During the eighteenth century therefore, almost all of the Dutch schools began to offer at least part of their instruction in English. By the American Revolution even the venerable Reformed Church School of New York City had allowed English into its classrooms.

The principal means of informal education underwent slight modification during English control over New York. The families of the colony's diverse national groups continued to offer their children their initial instruction in worldly matters in many tongues. In addition, the apprenticeship system under English rule remained the major source of vocational training for developing agricultural and commercial enterprises. In 1665 the "Duke's Laws" which first regulated the captured Dutch colony included a provision regarding apprenticeship. To some extent this provision copied existing New England statutes by requiring the instruction of all children and apprentices in "Matters of Religion and the Lawes of the Country . . . . and in some honest lawful calling labor or imployment." Unlike New England, however, the law provided no means of enforcement. Thus, the actual amount of education apprentices received in New York still depended largely on the terms of their indentures.

In the matter of formal learning, New York's colonial government assumed little responsibility aside from overseeing the training of pauper children and apprentices. Instructions to the colony's royal governors usually included the stipulation that they were to license all schoolmasters within their jurisdiction and that schoolmasters coming from England were also to be licensed by the Bishop of London. While the early royal governors proved rather conscientious about fulfilling this obligation, interest waned after the first decade of the eighteenth century. Educational efforts by the colonial assembly were also minimal. In 1691 and 1696 the legislature rejected two bills for founding schools, and the acts that were passed during the next century to encourage schools were "little more than hopeful gestures." Two assembly sponsored schools were founded in the eighteenth century, but these were short-lived. Thus, except for a few towns that maintained their own community schools, opportunities for formal education in New York rested in private hands.

At the elementary level such private education was dispensed by private tutors, private venture schools, or denominational institutions. The first method of learning, as in England and the southern colonies, was adopted by affluent upper-class parents. Private-venture schools, which were quite numerous in New York City, generally enrolled children from the middle classes. Exceptions to this general enrollment of middle-class children were the city's evening private schools where masters paid to have their apprentices learn elementary subjects in accordance with their indentures. Aside from this limited source of education for the lower classes, denominational institutions offered about the only other means of education for the colony's poor children. Several of New York's diverse religious sects offered such schooling, but it was the Episcopal Society for the Propagation of the Gospel in Foreign Parts that accomplished the most significant educational tasks during the colonial period.

The Society started its missionary and educational activities in New York in 1703. Three years later it began financial support for its schools in the colony with a gratuity of land and money voted to a Mr. William Huddleston who was appointed the Society's schoolmaster in New York City. In 1709, the S.P.G. aided the city's Trinity Church parish in founding a charity school, and by the close of the colonial period, the Society had established several similar institutions in towns throughout the colony. These year-round schools generally admitted a certain number of poor children *gratis* while they charged a small fee to other enrolled students. The number of poor children admitted was apparently small, since one writer noted in 1737 that most pauper children simply roamed the streets of New York. The subjects studied in these S.P.G. schools were reading, writing, and sometimes basic arithmetic. In addition, since the Society was an auxiliary of the Church of England, the students were also indoctrinated in Anglican ritual and the catechism. Textbooks were furnished by the Society, which also required annual progress reports from its appointed schoolmasters.

The S.P.G. also made notable efforts toward educating the colony's most debased social orders. In 1704 a catechizing school for Indians and Negroes was opened in New York City by Elias Neau, a Huguenot merchant. Neau had been persecuted and imprisoned in France for his religious beliefs, and in America he was motivated to aid the unfortunates who suffered because of their race. Despite considerable opposition and harassment, particularly from slave owners, Neau continued to operate his school until his death in 1722. Afterwards, his humanitarian work was continued by other Society appointees throughout New York Colony. None of his successors, however, equalled Neau's achievements and determination.

Even more than elementary education, secondary education in colonial New York existed almost exclusively on a private or parochial basis. The colonial legislature in 1702 enacted a law for the encouragement of a "Grammar Free-School in the City of New York," but the school which finally appeared two years later failed to survive to the end of the decade. In 1732 the Assembly adopted an act to establish a "public" grammar school whose masters would be appointed by civil authorities and paid from public taxes. The school had an advanced curriculum which included geometry, navigation, bookkeeping, and geography as well as the traditional classical studies. It led a tenuous existence, however, and was finally abandoned about 1738. Aside from the founding of a preparatory grammar school for King's College, New York's government gave no further assistance to secondary level education prior to the American Revolution. This field of learning was dominated by sectarian controlled institutions, private tutoring, and most especially by private venture schools.

New York's secondary level private venture schools were not unlike those in New England and the South. All of them were fee-paying institutions; they all offered instruction in a wide variety of subjects; they were usually individually operated, and were situated in urban centers. In New York these secondary private venture schools were located almost entirely in New York City and, as late as 1751, only a small minority of their masters were listed as "tolerably qualified." Most of New York's secondary private venture schools operated during the day for boys, though there were some evening private secondary schools, boarding schools, coeducational schools, and schools exclusively for girls. Such female institutions, however, were limited largely to the middle- and upper-class girls of New York City.

The colony's private venture secondary schools received sizable advertising in the local press. The following newspaper description in 1723 illustrates the broad curricular offerings and also indicates the relationship of these private schools to the academies which afterward emerged in Colonial America.

There is a School in New York, in the Broad Street, near the Exchange where Mr. John Walton, late of Yale-Colledge, Teacheth Reading, Writing, Arethmatick, whole Numbers and

Fractions, Vulgar and Decimal, the Mariners Art, Plain and Mercators Way; also Geometry, Surveying, the Latin Tongue, and Greek and Hebrew Grammars, Ethicks, Rhetorick, Logick, Natural Philosophy and Metaphysicks, all or any of them for a Reasonable Price. The School from the first of October till the first of March will be tended in the Evening. If any Gentlemen in the Country are disposed to send their Sons to the said School, if they apply themselves to the Master he will immediately procure suitable Entertainment for them, very cheap. Also if any Young Gentleman of the City will please to come in the Evening and make some Tryal of the Liberal Arts, they may have an opportunity of Learning the same Things which are commonly Taught in Colledges.

It was not until the final decades of the colonial period that New York established an institution of higher education. Before this period, the colony's few youths who wished to pursue studies beyond the secondary level either had to travel to one of the existing colonial colleges or else sail to Europe. Formal efforts to establish a college began during the 1740s and were led by the colonial legislature as well as permanent secular and religious residents of New York City. The proposal to found such a college, including the use of a fund-raising lottery, was approved in 1747. Considerable sums were raised during the next few years, but quarrels over the control and location of the proposed college among many of the colony's diverse religious sects delayed its opening. Finally, the disagreement was settled through the establishment of a nondenominational board of trustees and a provision that the college president must always be an Episcopalian. On July 17, 1754, King's College opened in New York City's Trinity Church with eight students and the Reverend Dr. Samuel Johnson as its president and sole faculty member.

During the subsequent two decades Kings College existed as a small, though liberally oriented, institution. By 1775 less than 200 students had been enrolled in the budding institution while less than 100 were listed as graduates. Under the presidency of Dr. Johnson the school followed its initial progressive declaration that "as to religion, there is no intent to impose on the scholars the peculiar tenets of any particular sect of Christians . . ." In this same announcement the college president proposed an advanced curriculum which would include "the arts of numbering and measuring, surveying and navigation, geography, history, husbandry, commerce, government, and the study of nature." While the impossibility of actually teaching such widely diversified studies led to the adoption of a generally traditional curriculum, the college nevertheless made some progressive moves within its course offerings. In 1757 it founded a professorship of mathematics and natural philosophy, in 1767 it organized a medical department, and in 1773 the college began its instruction in law. The American Revolution brought a temporary closing of the institution, but after the conflict it reopened with its new name, Columbia College.

Despite the various schools established in New York, education lagged under English rule. The government, for the most part, showed little interest in founding schools so that most poor children were dependent on the humanitarian efforts of religious denominations for the rudiments of learning. The work of the Episcopal S.P.G. was quite conspicuous in providing schooling for some underprivileged children; yet they performed their service at the cost of fixing the stigma of pauperism to free education. Since relatively few towns established their own schools, the principal source of elementary or secondary learning lay in private or denominational institutions. Illiteracy was consequently high in New York and its effects were clearly noted by the scientist Cadwallader Colden in 1750: "Tho the Province of New York abounds certainly more in riches than any other of the Northern Colonies, yet there has been less care to propagate knowledge or learning in it than anywhere else."

The Colony of New Jersey

The English seizure of New Netherlands in 1664 brought with it control of the territory between the lower Hudson River and the Delaware River. The region, which then contained only a few settlements of Dutch, Swedes, and Finns, was part of the land grant given to the Duke of York by Charles II. Shortly after receiving the extensive grant the Duke disposed of this particular area to two favorites, Lord John Berkeley and Sir George Carteret. These nobles were given title to the territory on a proprietary basis, and the region was named after Carteret's home on the channel island of Jersey. Seeking to attract new settlers to their holdings, the proprietors issued a document in 1665 that provided for low quitrents, a representative assembly, and liberty of conscience. At the same time, Philip Carteret, a relative of Sir George, was named governor and he proceeded to establish the capital of the province at Elizabethtown.

This original proprietorship over New Jersey did not last long. Despite the proprietors' liberal policies that encouraged immigration, the incoming settlers, particularly those from New England, proved restive under their absentee landlords. Many residents refused to pay any quitrents; they denied the authority of the proprietary government; and in 1672 they even expelled the legally appointed governor. Two years later, a discouraged Lord Berkeley sold his holdings to two Quakers and the colony was afterwards divided into two parts. Sir George Carteret retained the eastern section of the colony, but shortly after his death in 1679, his portion was also sold to a group of Quakers including William Penn. Finally, in 1702, the sections of East and West Jersey were united into one royal province, a status kept until the American Revolution.

Despite the union of East and West Jersey, many of the distinctions that marked these two sections continued throughout the colonial period. The bulk of the population remained in the eastern half of New Jersey, as did the majority of the colony's settlements. In addition, East Jersey reflected the small-farm characteristics from which many of its settlers came, while West Jersey contained plantations as well as small landholdings. During the eighteenth century divergent views between these two sections concerning landholding procedures even caused a split within the colonial legislature.

The principal economic occupation throughout all New Jersey was agriculture and the colony became known as the "garden of North America." Its farms produced grain, vegetables, cranberries, rice, and livestock. There was also a little manufacturing that centered around the production of pig iron, tar, pitch, resin, and other lumbering derivatives. Many of the agricultural and nonagricultural items produced in New Jersey were exported but, since the colony lacked an adequate commercial center, they were usually shipped abroad through New York or Philadelphia.

The social and religious features of colonial New Jersey were somewhat different from those of neighboring New York. New Jersey did have its upper-class aristocrats, but their number was far smaller than in the adjoining colony. As for the opposite end of its social structure, there were also far fewer slaves than in New York. The colony's diverse national-religious composition added another liberal feature to its development. Quakers, Puritans, Scotch-Irish Presbyterians, Dutch Reformed Churchmen, Anglicans, Baptists, and others practiced their beliefs within the colony. This broad diversity of sects produced a considerable degree of religious liberty, as well as the separation of church and state throughout all of New Jersey.

Education in New Jersey

Informal educational practices in New Jersey were similar to those in neighboring New York and Pennsylvania. The family group was generally the original source of instruction for the colony's diverse nationalities. This instructional role occurred particularly among the Scotch-Irish and New England Puritan settlers of New Jersey where families supplied their offspring with a basic elementary education when schools were unavailable. Apprenticeships were used as a means of vocational instruction by the colony's earliest settlers, and the practice was first regulated by the Quaker Assembly of West Jersey in 1682. Although no legislation was passed until 1774 requiring masters and mistresses to teach their apprentices reading and writing, many of the individual indentures contained a provision stipulating such instruction. Some denominations, such as the Quakers, provided a basic education for apprentices within their meetinghouses. Most of the colony's masters or mistresses, however, provided the requisite training for their apprentices by themselves.

The colony government made only a few early and abortive efforts to promote education. In 1682 the West Jersey Assembly granted the island of Matinicunk to the town of Burlington with the stipulation that any income from the island be used "for the maintaining of a school for the education of youth within the said town." Eleven years later an act was passed in East Jersey reflecting the influence of the New England settlers among its population. The act authorized the inhabitants of any town "to make a rate [tax] for the salary and maintaining of a schoolmaster within the said town for as long a time as they see fit." In 1695 the legislature acknowledged the apathy toward their previous legislation and delegated all educational responsibility to the towns. After the two Jerseys were united into a single royal province in 1702, no further attempts were made to establish a system of public schools. The government's interest in education was minimal, and even the governor's instructions to license all colony schoolmasters were usually ignored.

The Dutch instituted the first formal schooling in New Jersey. It began about 1661 or 1662 when the village of Bergen, opposite New Amsterdam, established a school. The school was operated much like the Dutch schools of New Netherlands and was maintained largely through taxes and fees. Its first school-masters also served as church clerks and court messengers. The Bergen school continued to function as a Dutch school until the eighteenth century when English was finally introduced. Although another Dutch school was founded in Hackensack about 1692, and some Reformed ministers and schoolmasters gave parochial instruction during the next century, the gradual assimilation of the Dutch into the English culture weakened the interest in a purely Dutch education.

Other religious sects in the colony also provided formal elementary level education. The New England Puritans who settled in eastern New Jersey appointed a schoolmaster for Newark in 1676, only 10 years after their arrival. Swedish settlers, who lived in West Jersey even before the English annexation, did not obtain the services of a regular school-master until 1714. New Jersey's Quaker-sponsored elementary schools were marked by advanced educational theories, al-though results were uneven. They intended their meeting house schools to train youth in ethics, practicality and piety, but their limited resources restricted their achievements. The first Episcopal school was opened in 1712 by the Reverend John Talbot, an S.P.G. missionary. This institution and similar schools subsequently founded by the Society in New Jersey were of the familiar charity-school variety. German Lutherans and Pietists also established schools in the colony during the eighteenth century, though most of them functioned on a some-what irregular basis. Baptists settled in New Jersey at the beginning of the eighteenth century, but according to one educational historian, it was not until about the middle of the century that they promoted elementary religious education. Finally, the numerous Scotch-Irish who settled New Jersey after 1700 were influenced by their strong belief in religious education to found schools. They established several elemen-tary level schools in the colony; among them was an Indian school opened early in 1746 at Crossweeksung by the Presby-terian missionary David Brainerd.

Besides these strictly denominational schools and the work of individual missionaries, there were a few other sources of elementary education. Private tutors were employed in New Jersey as early as 1679. Dame schools were introduced by New England settlers during the latter part of the seventeenth century. It was within these Puritan settlements of East Jersey that most of the colony's few semi-public schools were located in 1689. The town of Woodbridge opened a school supported by a land grant and town fees. A few other towns also established community schools, though maintaining them on a regular basis with competent masters proved difficult.

Opportunities for secondary education in colonial New Jersey were much fewer than for elementary instruction. Some religious denominations, including the Quakers, offered no schooling beyond the elementary level. Ministers or missionaries of some other sects also taught secondary level subjects on an individual or small group basis. The renewed religious zeal that emerged from the Great Awakening affected education and influenced denominations such as the Presbyterians and Congregationalists to found Latin Grammar schools. It was also partly as a result of this religious revival that the Baptists established a secondary level seminary at Hopewell in 1756. Because of the colony's lack of urban centers, private venture secondary schools usually found in the other middle colonies were lacking here, although Newark Academy was established shortly before the American Revolution. The proximity of New York City and Philadelphia, with their numerous academies and other private institutions, also attracted many affluent New Jersey youths seeking a secondary education.

It was in the realm of higher education that that colony made its most notable achievements. Prior to the American Revolution, New Jersey had founded two colleges—a greater number than in any other English colony in America.

The first of these colleges was established in 1746 and opened for instruction the following year. Its founders were New Light Presbyterian ministers who wanted an institution to train young men in their religious beliefs. Most of these ministers were also Yale graduates and their determination to found such an institution had increased after their alma mater had taken a distinctly antirevivalist Old Light position during the Great Awakening. Moves to obtain governmental approval for the college were undertaken in 1745 and, despite some opposition, a charter for the institution, known as the College of New Jersey, was granted by the governor the following year. In May, 1747 the school officially opened at Elizabethtown with eight or ten undergraduates under the presidency of the Reverend Jonathan Dickinson.

During the subsequent years preceding the American Revolution, the college experienced a period of growth and stability. After temporary placement in Elizabethtown and Newark, the school was given a permanent location at Princeton. There the college was renamed in honor of the townspeople's liberal donations and following the near completion of Nassau Hall, instruction began at Princeton in 1756. In addition to the local gifts, Princeton College also received financial benefactions from as far as Great Britain and obtained other income from colonial lotteries. The administrative leadership of the college also aided its early development. Despite the fact that several of its early presidents died after relatively brief tenure, they were able to place the college on solid footing. Princeton's low tuition charges and comparatively mild admissions requirements also increased its notoriety and students were attracted to the college from both New England and the South. By the American Revolution, the college enrollment had increased to almost 100 students.

Princeton College was directed largely along the traditional lines of older colonial colleges. It copied Yale's example of a single board of nonresident trustees, but while Presbyterian clergymen dominated this board at Princeton, membership also included other denominations.

The initial aim of the college, like other colonial schools, was the preparation of ministers, and one-half of Princeton's pre-Revolutionary graduates entered the clergy. Consequently, the original curriculum was classical and it was patterned after models already in use at Yale. A broadening of Princeton's curriculum to include' more secular studies occurred during the presidency of Samuel Davies (1759–1761), and, more particularly, during the tenure of the Reverend John Witherspoon (1768–1794). Yet by the end of the colonial period the course of study retained many traditional features. Student discipline still copied the familiar rigid patterns of other colonial schools. This evident fact was noted by a student who wrote in 1772 that two of his classmates were expelled "for stealing hens."

New Jersey's other colonial college received its first charter in 1766. The idea for this institution had been advanced during the previous decade by Dutch Reformed clergymen who were concerned about their continual supply of qualified ministers. Their success was achieved when New Jersey's royal governor chartered a school called Queen's College, honoring the wife of George III. Although the college board of trustees included governmental officials and other laymen as well as ministers, it was still more denominational than other contemporary colleges, and a second charter (1770) required the President to be a member of the Reformed Church. For a few years the College had only its charters to show its existence. Finally, in November 1771, the college opened for instruction in a former tavern in New Brunswick. The faculty of the school then consisted of only one teacher, and by the American Revolution Queens College enrolled only about 20 students. It was not until 1786 that the college finally obtained a regular president, and not until 1825 that it received the title Rutgers College.

Despite its distinction in higher education, the achievements in elementary and secondary education had lagged in colonial New Jersey. These levels of schooling were left in private hands with the government doing almost nothing on behalf of education. Although several religious sects filled the gap and actively promoted learning, particularly after the Great Awakening, the colonial period ended with a loose and unstructured pattern of schooling in the colony.

The Colony of Pennsylvania

The origins of Pennsylvania lay in the emergence of the religious sect known as The Friends or more commonly, Quakers. This Protestant denomination, which was founded in England about the middle of the seventeenth century, endorsed tenets that their contemporaries found radical and unsettling. Quakers had no ordained or paid ministry; they rejected all sacraments and ceremonies; they refused to take oaths or perform military service; and they were unwilling to pay taxes to an established church. They also believed that all men were equal in the sight of God and, therefore, they refused to acknowledge any differences in social rank. As a result of their extreme views, English Quakers suffered severe persecution during the rule of Oliver Cromwell and Charles II. Some of them migrated to America, but they found little spiritual freedom there. Finally, in 1681, the opportunity for a Quaker-administered refuge appeared when King Charles II granted an extensive proprietorship in America to William Penn, a Quaker convert who was the son of a former British admiral.

Penn intended his American colony to be a "Holy Experiment" with guaranteed religious freedom to all its settlers and a liberal form of government. He also wished the colony to be open to all peoples and he endeavored to induce immigrants from many Old World regions to migrate to Pennsylvania. The efforts of William Penn and his agents were successful. Attracted by the offers of religious liberty, democratic government and cheap fertile lands, settlers flocked to Pennsylvania from Germany, Holland, and France as well as from many parts of the British Isles. By the close of the colonial period Pennsylvania was the second most populous colony in English America. Its capital, Philadelphia, with a population of almost 40,000 in 1775, was the largest and probably most cosmopolitan community in the 13 colonies.

Despite his success in attracting settlers, William Penn proved unable to govern his proprietary province as smoothly as he had anticipated. He embodied his original ruling proposals in his first "Frame of Government," issued in 1682. This constitution provided for a bicameral legislature elected by the freeholders under liberal suffrage requirements. However, it also reserved to the proprietor or his selected governor the right to rule the colony and to reject all legislation. After Penn returned to England in 1684, the legislature attacked this ruling structure and the authority of appointed governors. Penn was unable to quell this increasing dissension and, from 1692 to 1696, his province was under royal control. When he regained authority over his colony, Penn tried to placate his critics in the legislature. The lower house, however, sought additional concessions, and by 1701 the first Frame of Government was abandoned, a unicameral legislature had been established, and the proprietor was left with only a veto power over legislation. That same year, William Penn left his colony for England where he died in 1718.

From Penn's death to the American Revolution, his province remained a proprietary colony though the proprietor's authority declined steadily. Not only did the eighteenth century proprietors have serious difficulty collecting quitrents on their lands, but they also had to fight the assembly's refusal to exempt their lands and income from taxation. The legislature itself was dominated by a conservative and affluent Quaker "party" until shortly after the middle of the century. This group was challenged and eventually ousted by a "popular" or "country" faction that supported the interests of small farmers and frontiersmen. In the final analysis, both the antiproprietary controversies and the legislative factionalism aided the colony's liberal political atmosphere. According to Max Savelle, "Pennsylvania enjoyed what was by far the most autonomous provincial government in all British America with the exception of Rhode Island and Connecticut."

The list of economic occupations in Pennsylvania was dominated by agriculture. Most of Pennsylvania's inhabitants were engaged in some form of agricultural activity on the colony's rich farmlands. Their bounteous production of grains and live-stock, exported in great quantity from Philadelphia, was a primary reason for the middle provinces earning the title "bread colonies." This extensive food production was re-flected in the growth of grist-mills in Pennsylvania to the sizable number of 83 by 1760. The colony's vast forests con-tributed to several industries, including lumbering, furniture-making and shipbuilding (considerable numbers of ships were constructed along the Delaware River). Philadelphia was also second only to New York as a market for western furs. In manufacturing, Pennsylvania led the colonies in the production of hats, and it also constructed the most iron furnaces and forges. Finally, there were many individual artisans and crafts-men as well as shopkeepers who operated successfully in Philadelphia and some of the other towns. Their occupations ranged from candlemaking to printing, but they all contributed to the colony's diverse and flourishing economy.

The religious pattern of the colony was marked by an atmos-phere of diversity and freedom. The Philadelphia region con-tained a particularly large number of faiths of which Quakers and Anglicans were generally the wealthiest and most in-fluential. Included among the many other denominations in this area were Baptists, Presbyterians, Lutherans, Huguenots, German Pietists, Catholics, and Jews. German Protestants, often referred to as "Pennsylvania Dutch," formed the principal denominations within the settlements adjoining the Phila-delphia region. Their numbers included Moravians, Mennonites, Schwenkfelders, Amish, and several other sects who had fled the recurrent wars and persecution in their homeland. Scotch-Irish Presbyterians were the main communicants in Penn-sylvania's frontier counties. These settlers had migrated to the colony primarily in the eighteenth century, and by the American Revolution they accounted for about one-third of its popula-tion. For all these creeds, religious liberty was a grant that had been maintained from Pennsylvania's early years of coloniza-tion. The absence of an established religion in the colony also aided its spirit of freedom and toleration.

Despite the fact that Quakers held advanced views on social democracy, a delineated class structure nevertheless emerged within colonial Pennsylvania. The top of this social structure was composed primarily of wealthy Quaker and Anglican merchants and landowners. Below this group was a much larger middle class of artisans, craftsmen, independent farmers, and tradesmen. The lower social orders were dominated by tenant farmers, unskilled laborers, indentured servants, and redemptioners. At the bottom of the class structure were the Negro slaves. Slaves constituted only a minute portion of the inhabitants, however, and by 1770 they amounted to less than 3 percent of Pennsylvania's entire population. Quaker opposition to chattel slavery was partially responsible for this low figure.

In the arts, Pennsylvania was one of the most advanced colonies in British America. The center of intellectual activity in the colony was Philadelphia. In addition to becoming a center of colonial writing and publishing, the city also contained many fine private literary collections, and in 1731 it chartered the Library Company of Philadelphia, the first of several subscription libraries in the colony. Interest was also shown in art, classical music (particularly among the Moravians), and in the theater, where the first professional company of actors in America was organized in Philadelphia in 1749. Scientific knowledge was promoted by men such as John Bartram, David Rittenhouse, John Logan, and Dr. John Morgan; but it was Benjamin Franklin who led the colony's intellectual activities. Franklin gained repute as a scientist, inventor, writer, and founder of the American Philosophical Society, and in education he provided extremely progressive concepts in learning.

Education in Colonial Pennsylvania

Quaker attitudes toward education had a prominent influence on Pennsylvania's initial actions concerning schooling. In this respect, it must be noted that the allegations of Quaker "antipathy" toward education by some historians are too generalized. While it is true that the Quakers, unlike the Puritans, did not believe that a classical education was essential for the ministry, and were also extremely critical of higher education, they nevertheless advocated training for all the youth in a community. Frederick Tolles, a historian of the American Quakers, pointed out that the schooling then proposed for children was based on realistic new educational theories that were designed "to replace the traditional classical tradition." These progressive concepts, he noted, emphasized an "empirical and utilitarian" approach to education at the expense of the "dialectical and humanistic." In following this educational philosophy, the Friends' schools, which were founded in seventeenth-century England, offered religious instruction, moral training, and also practical learning that would enable the student to earn a livelihood. Such elementary level schools were made available to all Quaker children without restriction.

William Penn reflected much of this Quaker educational philosophy. Although he had attended Oxford, Penn did not refrain from condemning the English universities as "Signal Places for Idleness, Looseness, Prophaness, and gross Ignorance." Yet despite this strong criticism of existing classical higher education, Penn himself did not reject all forms of learning. He promoted instead the Friends' emphasis on practical education. In his writings he argued that children should be allowed to cultivate their "natural genius to mechanical and physical or natural knowledge" rather than being stuffed with "words and rules to know grammar, rhetoric, and a strange tongue or two." For his own children's education, Penn was more specific: "I recommend the useful parts of mathematics, as building houses or ships, measuring surveying, dialing, navigation; but agriculture especially is my eye. Let my children be husbandmen and housewives; it is industrious, healthy and of good example." All learning, he concluded, should be made "easy and cheerful, without much fierceness or beating."

The progressive educational concepts of William Penn and

his Quaker brethren were incorporated into some of Pennsylvania's earliest legislation. Penn believed that a free government must look after the education of its youth so that they should be able afterwards to rule with wisdom and virtue. In this respect the colony's first General Assembly provided in its "Great Law" of 1682, that the "Laws of this Province . . . shall be one of the books taught in the schools of this Province and territories thereof." The next year the Assembly adopted Penn's second Frame of Government containing a more specific educational provision:

And to the end that poor as well as rich may be instructed in good and commendable learning, which is to be preferred before wealth, Be it enacted, etc., That all persons in this Province and Territories thereof, having children, and all guardians and trustees of orphans, shall cause such to be instructed in reading and writing, so that they may be able to read the Scriptures and to write by the time they attain to twelve years of age; and that then they be taught some useful trade or skill, that the poor may work to live, and the rich if they become poor may not want: of which every County Court shall take care. And in case such parents, guardians, or overseers shall be found deficient in this respect, every such parent, guardian, or overseer shall pay for every such child, five pounds, except there should appear an incapacity in body or understanding to hinder it.

Despite such progressive actions, the colony did not develop a system of government-supported, free, public education. Penn's first Frame of Government had provided that the "governor and Provincial Council shall erect and order all publick schools." Although Penn and his council used this provision in 1683 to invite Enoch Flower to become Philadelphia's first schoolmaster, and although some elementary schools were founded with state assistance, little was actually done to enforce the existing educational statutes throughout Pennsylvania. Several factors accounted for this lack of enforcement in the colony. Among them were the national and religious diversities of Pennsylvania's inhabitants, the political opposition to proprietary rule, and the general unwillingness of the inhabitants to devote as much of their children's time as Penn considered necessary for education. Even the proprietor's initial scheme to promote schools by refusing to allow settlers to acquire land except in townships was soon abandoned. In 1693 the comprehensive school law adopted 10 years before was reenacted, but it quickly became a dead letter. The Charter of Privileges of 1701 failed to mention education, and during the subsequent years prior to the American Revolution, the colony largely abandoned formal education to parochial or private efforts.

As for informal educational procedures, Pennsylvania, like other Middle Colonies, left the first and foremost responsibility with individual families. Quakers, desirous of imbuing their children with their particular sentiments on theology, moral behavior, and practicality believed that the home was an initial starting-point for such teachings. They sought to be broadminded in this home training, and as one Quaker schoolmaster stated, "We deny nothing for children's learning that may be honest and useful . . . ." German Pietists in the colony also stressed informal home instruction although their teachings tended to be more rigid and sectarian than in Quaker families. Along the frontier—especially where schools were not immediately available—the Scotch-Irish relied extensively on family instruction for teaching children.

The other means of informal education in the colony came through apprenticeship. In 1682, the Pennsylvania legislature enacted its first apprenticeship statute that obligated masters to make certain that their apprentices were "able to read the Scriptures, and to write by the time they attain to twelve years of age." Although this law soon became inoperative, it did reflect the emphasis that the founders of the colony placed on vocational education. In 1693 the legislature's upper house permitted the Quakers to establish a "school where poor children may be freely maintained, taught, and educated in good literature, until they be fit to be put out as apprentices." This preapprenticeship schooling formed the basis for many Quaker charity schools. During the succeeding years prior to the American Revolution, apprenticeship legislation was minimal and centered primarily on the means of binding out specific groups of unfortunate children.

Formal elementary instruction in Pennsylvania originated in 1683 when Governor Penn and his Council invited Enoch Flower to establish a school in Philadelphia for the teaching of reading, writing, and casting accounts. Flower, an experienced English schoolmaster, opened his school soon afterwards, charging fees to all students except the poor. The school proved quite popular during its early years and it even attracted students from outside the colony. Influenced by Flower's successful work Thomas Budd, a prominent Quaker, proposed in 1685 that "public" schools with masters chosen by the governor and legislature be provided in all communities. Budd's proposals, however, like the educational efforts of William Penn proved fruitless in the face of the colonists preference for denominational or private control over learning.

Of all the denominations the colony's Quakers probably performed the most significant endeavors at the elementary level of learning. Here the basic formal schooling furnished by the Friends coincided with their previously mentioned emphasis on practical knowledge as well as their inherent liberalism and humanitarianism. In these respects the curriculum in their lower schools generally consisted of reading, writing, casting accounts, and ciphering. Both sexes were offered such training equally, and the Friends' schools usually admitted poor children without tuition charges. Some Negroes were also educated in these Quaker schools or in Quaker homes, and in 1700 a school for black children was founded in Philadelphia by prominent Friends. (Teaching of Indians was also urged by many Quakers though most of these natives proved suspicious of the white man's learning.) All these Quaker schools were under the supervision of the Society's Monthly Meetings, so the schoolmaster was usually a member of the denomination. Despite this parochial management, Quaker-sponsored elementary schools flourished, and by the middle of the eighteenth century, according to Dr. Thomas Woody, there were about 40 such institutions in Pennsylvania.

Other religious denominations also established elementary level schools in the colony. The Episcopal Society for the Propagation of the Gospel in Foreign Parts founded a number of charity schools in the Philadelphia region, including a school for Negroes. In the same area other denominational sects established lower level schools for their children. In interior counties, settled principally by German immigrants, parochial schools were also established. Although most of these German settlers displayed little interest in founding schools and promoting formal learning, the Moravian immigrants proved a distinct exception. Among the numerous elementary level schools which they opened was a "nursery school" at Nazareth, which some historians consider the first infant school in America. During the 1750s and early 1760s several hundred German boys were also given a rudimentary education in charity schools established by the Episcopal "Society for the Propagation of Christian Knowledge among the Germans in America." Finally, in the frontier countries of western Pennsylvania, the Scotch-Irish Presbyterians founded many elementary-level schools for their children.

From its earliest years of settlement, Pennsylvania had schoolmasters who taught elementary subjects on a private basis. Christopher Taylor, a learned Quaker, conducted a school on Tinicum Island in about 1684, and Benjamin Clift opened a private school in Delaware County in 1692. By the eighteenth century, the colony's greatest concentration of such private elementary schools was in Philadelphia where they thrived alongside existing denominational institutions. Some of these lower schools were of the dame-school variety, some were boarding schools, and some were coeducational, while others limited their enrollment by sex. Regardless of their makeup however, these private elementary schools contributed to Philadelphia's extensive educational opportunities.

Despite the overall pattern of parochial or private control of education, there were a few settlements in the colony which had community-controlled elementary schools. One area where this occurred was the Wyoming Valley which was settled by Connecticut emigrants during the last decades of the colonial period. Also in the later colonial era, a few Quaker schools were taken over and converted into community schools. Both these instances, however, were exceptional deviations from the generally private or parochial control of elementary education in Pennsylvania.

Formal secondary education began soon after the founding of Pennsylvania and it followed similar patterns of control as in elementary education. In 1689 the Philadelphia Monthly Meeting of Friends established a public grammar school and appointed Mr. George Keith as its master. The school, known originally as the "Friends Public School" and later as the William Penn Charter School, was open to the children of the community, but tuition charges were assessed on all except poor children. Keith taught his students Latin along with other secondary subjects, and in 1690 he was given an usher to help instruct the growing number of students. In 1697 this popular institution was incorporated by the Pennsylvania Council, and in 1701 it was officially chartered by Penn himself. While the Friends Public School was open to all children, it nevertheless was maintained under the denominational supervision of the Quakers.

Several other secondary level denominational schools were founded in the colony prior to the American Revolution. Episcopalians in Philadelphia established a parish school that by the eighteenth century was dispensing some instruction in Latin. Other parochial schools in the community also gave classical training. Among the German settlers outside Philadelphia, the Moravians performed singular work. This sectarian group operated a secondary-level boarding school for girls at Bethlehem, and also stressed the teaching of sacred music in their curriculum. The Scotch-Irish Presbyterians founded several secondary level schools including the so-called "Log College" opened by the Reverend William Tennent at Nashiminy in 1726. The school, which functioned until Tennent's resignation in 1742, was designed for training future Presbyterian ministers and its closing influenced the subsequent founding of Princeton College. Another notable Presbyterian institution was the Reverend Francis Alison's New London grammar school opened in 1743. The Quakers, as already noted, had founded the Friends Public School, but their general disdain toward classical learning limited their activity in opening schools at the secondary level.

Pennsylvania also had a number of privately maintained secondary schools during the later colonial period. Most of these institutions were concentrated in Philadelphia and had curricula offerings as widely varied as those in similar schools in other colonial cities. Private schoolmasters, such as Andrew Lamb, George Brownell, and William Robbins offered instruction in courses including "Navigation, Gauging, Merchants Accompts, Geometry, Trigonometry, Surveying, French, Spanish, Latin, and Greek." The most diversified school curriculum however, was advertised for the opening of Benjamin Franklin's Philadelphia Academy in 1751. Besides the previously mentioned subjects, Franklin's academy offered instruction in such fields as history, government, economics, literature, drawing, and composition.

In addition to these daytime secondary schools, the city also had several evening schools where workmen and artisans might acquire vocational skills or gain advanced training. Philadelphia also had among the finest educational opportunities for young girls and, according to Carl Bridenbaugh, it had the best girls' school in the colonies which was opened by David James Dove. Young girls in the city were known to receive training not only in domestic subjects, but also in advanced arithmetic and foreign languages.

Philadelphia's excellent educational opportunities of all varieties even attracted students from outside the colony and may have influenced the following doggerel of one prominent resident:

> *Here are schools of divers sorts,*
> *To which our youth daily resorts,*
> *Good women, who do very well*
> *Bring little ones to read and spell*
> *Which fits them for writing, and then,*
> *Here's men to bring them to their pen,*
> *And to instruct and make them quick*
> *In all sorts of Arithmetick.*

In addition to the schoolmasters already mentioned, Pennsylvania had other educators of note. One of them was Anthony Benezet, a Philadelphia Quaker who was a prominent advocate of kindness, patience, and understanding for schoolmasters. Benezet himself began his lengthy teaching career at the Penn Charter School in 1742 and later founded a girls' school that had a progressively oriented curriculum. Another noteworthy schoolmaster was Francis Pastorius, a scholarly German Pietist who had been educated at some of the best European universities. Pastorius, an advocate of the traditional stern classroom discipline, taught at the Penn Charter School from 1698 to 1700 and later taught the classics at his own school in Germantown until shortly before his death in 1720. An even more distinguished German schoolmaster in colonial America was Christopher Dock, the "pious schoolmaster on the Skippack." Dock emigrated to Pennsylvania about 1710, established a school for Mennonites a few years later, and continued teaching until his death in 1771. His place in education was marked by many progressive and humanitarian concepts but most prominently by the publication in 1770 of his *Schulordnung*, the first American treatise on schoolkeeping.

Another Pennsylvanian, who was not a schoolmaster but nevertheless contributed very significant educational concepts, was the illustrious Benjamin Franklin. Franklin was a product of the new American middle class, and his concepts reflected the realistic perspective of this group. In this respect Franklin expressed himself as a reformer who stressed a utilitarian and nonsectarian approach to education. He rejected the traditional accent on religious orthodoxy and classical indoctrination and substituted instead his belief in a program of studies that met the actual needs of colonial society. An upper-level school curriculum, in his opinion, should include moral instruction and, more importantly, it should be broad enough to train boys for any profession or trade. This observation is reflected in the following excerpt from Franklin's *Proposals Relating to the Education of Youth in Pennsylvania* (1749), a work that expressed much of his philosophy of learning:

As to their studies, it would be well if they could be taught everything that is useful and everything that is ornamental: but art is long, and their time is short. It is therefore proposed that they learn those things that are likely to be most useful and most ornamental. Regard being had to the several professions for which they are intended.

All should be taught to write a fair hand, and swift, as that is useful to all. And with it may be learnt something of drawing, by imitation of prints, and some of the first principles of perspective. Arithmetic, accounts, and some of the first principles of geometry and astronomy. The English language might be taught by grammar; in which some of our best writers, as Tillotson, Addison, Pope, Algernon Sidney, Cato's Letters, etc. should be classics. The style principally to be cultivated, being the clear and the concise. Reading should also be taught, and pronouncing, Properly, distinctly, emphatically, not with an even tone, which under-does, nor a theatrical, which over-does nature.

To form their style they should be put on writing letters to each other, making abstracts of what they read or writing the same things in their own words; telling or writing stories lately read, in their own expressions. All to be revised and corrected by the tutor who should give his reasons, explain the force and import of words, etc. . . . . . .

Benjamin Franklin was also instrumental in the founding of the College of Philadelphia. After the Philadelphia Academy had opened in 1751, Franklin believed that this institution should soon develop into a "regular college." The opportunity for establishing such a college came two years later, after the Academy had obtained the right to grant college degrees and after Franklin had read William Smith's pamphlet, *A General Idea of the College of Mirania*. Smith, a graduate of the University of Aberdeen who was then teaching in New York, had advocated a practical type of higher education aimed at producing a wise and useful citizenry. These ideas intrigued Franklin so much that he invited the Scotch schoolmaster to Philadelphia to meet the other proponents of a college. Smith impressed these Philadelphians and in May 1755, he was confirmed as provost of the newly chartered "College, Academy, and Charitable School of Philadelphia."

During the next twenty years, the College of Philadelphia (later the University of Pennsylvania) remained a small, but progressive institution. Although Provost Smith had advocated the projected nondenominational control of the College, it soon came under Episcopal domination, and Smith himself became a target of considerable criticism. This factor, as well as the Quaker animosity toward higher education, helped limit the total student enrollment. Nevertheless, the college took some forward-looking steps prior to the American Revolution. Provost Smith introduced a liberal three-year undergraduate curriculum that emphasized not only the classics but also mathematics, philosophy, oratory, and the natural and social sciences. Later, in 1765, Dr. John Morgan established a medical school in connection with the college. The College of Philadelphia then became the first institution in the colonies to appoint a professor of chemistry; the man selected for this work was the eminent Dr. Benjamin Rush, an advocate of many of Franklin's liberal educational ideals.

The achievements of the College of Philadelphia represented only part of the many educational advances made by the colony of Pennsylvania. These advances were made at all levels of learning and were promoted by some of the most prominent schoolmasters and educational theorists in colonial America. Government in Pennsylvania did not take a determinative role in education, however, and the successes that were made in learning were accomplished under private or parochial direction. This factor, of course, restricted the forms and availability of education. Nevertheless, the principal patterns of education that were established in colonial Pennsylvania were to continue until well into the nineteenth century.

Delaware

The history of Delaware Colony included years of Swedish, Dutch, and English control. Although the Dutch made the initial attempt to found an outpost within this region, the first successful move to establish a permanent settlement there was made by the Swedes. This settlement, which was promoted by the Swedish West India Company in 1638, was named Fort Christina, and the colony itself was called New Sweden. Few emigrants came to the colony, however, and its general lack of support from the homeland weakened New Sweden to such an extent that the Dutch had little difficulty seizing the territory in 1655. Dutch control lasted less than a decade. With the English conquest of New Netherlands in 1664, these lands came under the rule of the Duke of York. New Amstel, the principal Dutch settlement, was now called New Castle; Fort Christina became Wilmington; and the entire region was known as Delaware, or "the Territories." In 1682, the Duke granted the three counties comprising this region to William Penn and they were subsequently incorporated into the province of Pennsylvania. Then, in 1703, Delaware organized its own independent legislature, though until the American Revolution its governor was the executive of Pennsylvania.

During the colonial period, Delaware remained a thinly settled region of diverse inhabitants with strong ties to neighboring Pennsylvania province. By 1770, Delaware had only 35,496 inhabitants—far less than the three other middle colonies. In addition to the Swedes and Finns who first settled there, the colony also contained Dutch, Scotch-Irish, German, and English settlers, plus a relatively small number of Negro slaves. This diversity of national stocks, as in Pennsylvania, led to a considerable degree of toleration and the absence of an established church in the colony. Delaware's predominant economic occupation was agriculture, and, though the colony did include one estate of 24,000 acres, most farms were small and operated without servants or slaves. Since the colony had few sizable settlements its agricultural produce was exported almost exclusively from Philadelphia. Delaware's tiny upper class also looked outward to Philadelphia as its social center.

Education in Delaware

Delaware's governmetal actions toward education, as well as its patterns of informal education, were often entwined with those of Pennsylvania. From 1682 to 1703 the educational legislation enacted by the Pennsylvania legislature was directly binding upon Delaware's three counties. It also meant that Pennsylvania's general legislative inaction toward education after 1683, and its subsequent abandonment of educational responsibility to private or denominational groups, affected Delaware too. The perpetuation of this educational situation was evident in a Delaware statute of 1743, which resembled an earlier Pennsylvania law (1731) that confirmed religious bodies in their right to maintain schools and in the possession of all property raised or given for this purpose. Apprenticeship practices were also similar to Pennsylvania's. The Pennsylvania apprenticeship statute of 1683 set the model for Delaware, and there were a few charity schools that offered some apprentices rudimentary learning.

The first school in Delaware was opened by the Dutch. The charter of the patroon of New Amstel in 1656 had provided that the city of Amsterdam would "send thither a proper person for schoolmaster," and would temporarily provide the salary for "said schoolmaster." By 1657 a school was formally operating in the community although its handicaps were illustrated in a letter the schoolmaster sent to Holland: "I am engaged in keeping school, with twenty-five children in it, but I have no paper nor pens for the use of the children, nor slates and pencils." This elementary level school continued to operate throughout the period of Dutch control over Delaware.

Other national groups in the colony were slower to provide formal learning. Though the Swedes had made a few efforts to establish schools, even before the Dutch conquest, the records indicate that it was not until 1699 that they hired their first schoolmaster. When the three Delaware counties came under the control of Pennsylvania, English settlers who wished to provide education outside the home initially would send their children to Philadelphia for schooling.

During the first three-quarters of the eighteenth century, a number of new elementary level schools were established in the colony, primarily by religious denominations. After hiring their first schoolmaster in 1699, the Swedish congregation at Christina maintained a school on an irregular basis until 1759. The first school that the Quakers established in the colony was at Wilmington in 1748. Episcopal missionaries, such as George Ross at New Castle and Thomas Crawford at Dover, did their best to provide education for the lower social orders in the colony. Most of the teaching these S.P.G. missionaries provided was nevertheless of the sectarian, charity school variety. In 1734 a schoolmaster named John Russell was mentioned in the town records of Lewes, although a schoolhouse was not listed until 1761. Private elementary schools or old field schools of the southern style were established occasionally in Delaware, and these sometimes were taught by indentured servants. Basically, however, elementary education in the colony was denominational and the level of literacy remained low.

Formal secondary level instruction in Delaware did not commence until well into the eighteenth century and, prior to the American Revolution, it was available on a very limited basis. An academy was founded in Wilmington about 1765 with the support of several prominent community leaders. Also in Wilmington, a Scotchman named Mr. Wilson maintained a school for both sexes as early as 1760, though he restricted the girls' education to the basic rudiments. However, the most notable pre-Revolutionary secondary school in Delaware was Newark Academy. The Academy had its origins in the Reverend Francis Alison's Pennsylvania grammar school that, after 1752, was directed by the Reverend Alexander McDowell. McDowell moved this Presbyterian institution first to Elkton, Maryland and finally, in 1767, to Newark where the Academy continued its notable work. Other than these aforementioned examples, the only other means of obtaining secondary training within the colony was through individual tutoring.

No institutions of higher education were founded in Delaware during the colonial period. Newark Academy probably provided a basis for the establishment of Delaware College, but this occurred well after the American Revolution. For the few residents of the colony who sought higher level instruction, the College of Philadelphia was the most convenient, and one of the least expensive, institutions.

*   *   *   *

Several conclusions come from this survey of education in the Middle Colonies. First, the overall growth of formal learning developed rather slowly. Most of the region's secondary and higher level institutions were not established until the last three decades of the colonial period. Second, the Middle Colonies had displayed a drift away from a state-regulated school system toward denominational or family responsibility for learning. Third, the region had been able to establish some of the most varied and progressive educational institutions in the English colonies, despite governmental indifference to formal instruction. Examples of such progressive learning were evident at the College of Philadelphia, Kings College, the Philadelphia Academy, Francis Alison's Grammar school, and other private or sectarian institutions. Fourth, the Middle Colonies were also noteworthy for their progressive educational theorists such as William Penn, Christopher Dock, Samuel Davies, and Benjamin Franklin. Finally, it was within the secondary and higher level educational institutions of this colonial section that the initial movements began away from the Old World accent on academic custom and religious orthodoxy to a more realistic and nonsectarian approach to education. In this respect, the Middle Colonies probably made their greatest contribution to the future of American education.

epilogue

This book examined the origins and development of educational practices in the New England, Southern, and Middle Colonies. The first settlers in each of these colonial sections attempted to transplant the more-familiar learning practices of their homeland to the American wilderness. The New World environment served to alter or restrict the extent of this educational transplantation. The result was the inevitable breakdown of many traditional European learning patterns and their transformation into new colonial educational practices that tried to meet the needs and desires of the individualistic eighteenth-century Americans. By the time of the American Revolution this transformation had become evident throughout the colonies.

In 1776, some vestiges of the educational theories and practices of seventeenth-century colonists still remained, although their extent and influence was limited. These traces of earlier learning patterns were exhibited in several aspects of elementary and secondary schooling: the continuance of apprenticeship systems, the survival of endowed schools and Latin grammar schools, the persistence of sectarian influences and outdated pedagogical procedures, the generally circumscribed and debased condition of the teaching profession, and the general obstacles to educational attainment based upon race, religion, sex, or social standing. In higher education these vestiges were manifested in such factors as sectarianism, classicism, and rigid codes for student conduct.

Yet, despite the persistence of earlier educational practices, colonial society by 1776 had evolved to such an extent that American education was now directed toward more realistic and utilitarian goals. This new trend was apparent in practices such as the prevalent adoption of arithmetic in elementary instruction, the development of a more broadly based curriculum for secondary instruction, and the emergence of the academy and other institutions to serve as private vocational schools. Educational change was also evident at the college level where the curriculum expanded from its narrow classical foundations, professional training in law and medicine was offered, and control over these higher institutions began to shift from its circumscribed denominational base.

As the colonial period ended, these and other changes had not only brought vast diversification to American education, but also had made it far more responsive to the heterogeneous society that it served. Several obstacles to the completion of this educational transformation remained for some time, of course, and were not eradicated until the Revolutionary Period (1776-1789). A few more hindrances even lasted until well into the nineteenth century. Nevertheless, the origins of educational change and development in the United States are rooted in the years from 1607 to 1776. Their results have influenced the course of American schooling—even to the present.

bibliographical essay